Teach Yourself English

Preparation
For English
Proficiency
Examinations

by **Wm. L. Young**

PROFESSOR EMERITUS OF ENGLISH
CAPITAL UNIVERSITY/OHIO

Barron's Educational Series, Inc.
Woodbury, New York

Introduction

How good are you in English?

Why not take our test and see.

I. **The Trial Test**

On page 3, answer all thirty-two items of the TRIAL TEST by placing an R in the parentheses if the item is right and W if it is wrong.

II. **Scoring**

Now, for the first time, use our interesting and easy device for self-teaching:

Bend page 3 so your answers line up and match the right answers on page 5.

Place an X before each item missed on page 3 and record in the blank at the bottom of the page the total wrong.

III. **Interpretation**

If you missed none or only one—Congratulations! Maybe you don't need this book!

If you missed only two, you are good!

If you missed three or more—Ouch!—surely you need more study, and this is the book that can help you; so

LOOK AT PAGE 3 AND GET TO WORK!

©1968 by Barron's Educational Series, Inc.

All rights are strictly reserved.

Library of Congress Catalog Card No. 68-8682 *ap 11'78*

PRINTED IN THE UNITED STATES OF AMERICA

11 M 9 8 7

Trial Test

Test Yourself: Place R in the parentheses if right; W, if wrong.
Example: He brung me the book. (W)

1. I was lying on the couch. ( )
2. Mathematics is important for the engineer. ( )
3. I beleive you recieved my letter. ( )
4. Tom Jones, a freshman, is the president of his class. ( )
5. The work he done was difficult. ( )

6. It travels the smoke further. ( )
7. I will compel him! He shall help me! ( )
8. This was my most unique experience. ( )
9. Select whomever you wish. ( )
10. Set on the stove and stir occasionally. ( )

11. He asked Jim, "Why did your brother quit?" ( )
12. I love a ball game, swimming and to ski. ( )
13. It tastes like a cigarette should. ( )
14. He feels sorry about losing the game. ( )
15. Playing, running, shouting, and leaping on the campus. ( )

16. Us freshmen should get better treatment. ( )
17. Data are difficult to gather. ( )
18. Yesterday he lay there for an hour. ( )
19. There was no one there except him and I. ( )
20. Everyone should do their duty. ( )

21. Neither the boys nor their leader was aware of this fact. ( )
22. To be well-cooked, you must boil the broth an hour. ( )
23. He asked me to immediately and definitely answer. ( )
24. The principle of the school tried to seperate them. ( )
25. These are the colors of the flag; red, white and blue. ( )

26. We praise these kind of students. ( )
27. There was many causes for this action. ( )
28. This is he. ( )
29. They asked him during the next month to take his vacation. ( )
30. That evening he called for my girl had told me. ( )
31. To know him was to love him. ( )
32. The boy stood on the burning deck
    Whence all but him had fled. ( )

Number wrong

COMMENT: If you missed three or more, don't be discouraged, for we are here to help you. Later we shall test you again. But if you do need help,

TURN THE PAGE AND START YOUR STUDY!

[3]

Hints: Parts of Speech — Grammar

1.0 PARTS OF SPEECH. There are 450,000 words in the latest unabridged dictionary of our language. All of these fall into eight classes called Parts of Speech. Sometimes you will make mistakes in English because you use the wrong part of speech. Therefore, it is important that you know and recognize each kind. These eight parts of speech are noun, pronoun, verb, adjective, adverb, preposition, conjunction, and interjection.

1.1 A NOUN is the name of something. *John, home, tree* are nouns.

1.2 A PRONOUN is a word used instead of a noun. This noun is called the *antecedent*. *He, they, who, it, this* are pronouns.

1.3 A VERB expresses action or state of being. He *runs.* She *is* a lady. He *seems* happy. The book *was closed.*

1.4 AN ADJECTIVE modifies a noun or pronoun (It modifies if it describes, limits, or restricts). I saw a *beautiful* flower (describes). Pick the *seventh* member (restricts).

1.5 AN ADVERB modifies a verb, adjective, or another adverb. He ran *rapidly* (modifies a verb). He ran *very* rapidly (modifies another adverb). She sang a *very* beautiful song (modifies an adjective).

1.6 A PREPOSITION is a word used before a noun or pronoun to show its relationship to some other word. He went *to* town. He looks *like* me. All went *except* me. He asked *for* help.

1.7 A CONJUNCTION connects words or groups of words. *And, if, or, as, unless, but* are some of the conjunctions.

1.8 AN INTERJECTION is a word expressing strong or sudden feeling. *Alas, hurrah, lo, ha, fie, pshaw, whoopee* are interjections.

Hint 1. Judge Parts of Speech by their use.
Usage determines what part of speech a word is. Change its job and you change its class:
Noun: The *outside* of the book is black.
Adjective: The *outside* cover is black.
Preposition: He went *outside* the yard.
Adverb: He went *outside.*

Well may be noun, adjective, or adverb: The *well* is deep (noun); Are you *well* again? (adjective); He did *well* (adverb). *Good* is never an adverb: Wrong: He sang *good;* He did *good* (Use *well* instead of *good*). *Like* is never a conjunction. It may be a noun, verb, adjective, or preposition. Wrong: He did *like* you said. Right: He did *as* you said. Noun: His *like* is rare. Verb: I *like* him. Adjective: We have *like* tastes. Preposition: She looks *like* her mother.

NOW DO THE EXERCISE ON PAGE 5

Exercise 1

Trial I   IDENTIFY the italicized word by writing its number in the proper parentheses (1. noun; 2. pronoun; 3. adjective; 4. adverb; 5. verb; 6. preposition; 7. conjunction; 8. interjection):

Right answers for page 3 | Your answers for page 5

1. Truth crushed to earth shall rise *again*.   R   ( )
2. Is this the face that *launched* a thousand ships?   R   ( )
3. *Oh,* what shall I do!   W   ( )
4. *Seven* is a lucky number.   R   ( )
5. *Seven* ducks arose from the swamp.   W   ( )
6. Either you *or* I should go.   ( )
7. *They* visited in our city.   W   ( )
8. The world will not see his *like* again.   R   ( )
9. He looks *like* his father.   W   ( )
10. *Like* conditions produce *like* results.   R R   ( )

In the following items, place R if right, W if wrong:

R

11. He sure sings beautiful.   W   ( )
12. He drives carefully.   W   ( )
13. No one came but he.   R   ( )
14. This milk tastes sourly.   W   ( )
15. He plays tennis well.   ( )

W

CHECK your answers with the key on page 7. If all are correct, pat yourself on the back and move ahead by turning immediately to page 6. However, if you miss one or more, re-study page 4 and then try

R R W W

Number wrong

Trial II   IDENTIFY the italicized words by placing in the proper parentheses its number as stated above.

R W

1. *Strike* while the iron is hot.   W   ( )
2. Take Time *by* the forelock.   W   ( )
3. Love all, trust a few, do *wrong* to none.   W   ( )
4. Both you *and* I should pay.   ( )
5. *I* am eager to visit Boston.   W   ( )
6. Write *carefully*.   W   ( )
7. The *well* is sixty feet deep.   R   ( )
8. A *well* person would never do that.   W   ( )
9. *Well,* now what shall we do?   W   ( )
10. He always does *well* on tests.   R   ( )

In the following place R if right and W if wrong.

R

11. He sure knows his stuff.   ( )
12. Velvet feels smooth.   ( )
13. No one knew the answer but he.   ( )
14. This rose smells sweetly.   ( )
15. How fragrant these flowers smell.   ( )

CHECK your answers as before. On Trial II be satisfied with only a perfect score. If you miss one or more, erase all your answers, or cover them with a slip of paper, re-study, and re-take all parts until there is COMPLETE MASTERY. AFTER MASTERY, STUDY HINTS ON PAGE 6

Number wrong

[5]

Hints: The Sentence — Grammar

2.0 THE SENTENCE. A sentence is the expression of a thought.
2.1 It must have a subject and a predicate.
2.2 The subject names that about which something is thought. Examples: The *lady* wrote me a letter. The tall *tree* is beautiful.
2.3 The predicate names what is thought of the subject. *Lady* is the simple subject; *the lady* is the complete subject; *wrote* is the simple predicate; *wrote me a letter* is the complete predicate.
2.4 The subject may be compound: *The boys and girls* studied. The predicate may be compound: They will *shout, sing,* and *dance*.
2.5 KINDS OF SENTENCES—ACCORDING TO MEANING.
    2.51 DECLARATIVE (a statement). He is a friend of mine. (Use period at the end)
    2.52 INTERROGATIVE (a question). What did he do? (Use question mark at the end)
    2.53 IMPERATIVE (a command). Do your duty! (Use exclamation point if strong; period, if not)
    2.54 EXCLAMATORY (strong feeling). Alas! What shall I do! (Use exclamation point)
2.6 KINDS OF SENTENCES—ACCORDING TO STRUCTURE.
A clause is a sentence or a part of a sentence containing a subject and a predicate. Clauses are main (or independent); subordinate (or dependent). In the sentence, He who runs may read, *He may read* is the main clause, and *who runs* is the subordinate.
    2.61 SIMPLE (one main clause): The birds twitter.
    2.62 COMPOUND (two or more main clauses): The birds twitter and the flowers bloom.
    2.63 COMPLEX (one main clause and one or more dependent clauses): When I am happy, I sing.
    2.64 COMPOUND-COMPLEX (two or more main clauses and one or more dependent clauses): If you are happy and free from care, the world seems bright and cheerful, and everybody seems to be your friend.

Hint 2. In every sentence look for a subject and a predicate, expressed or unexpressed.
Sometimes the subject or predicate may be unexpressed but understood as in the imperative sentence: Go (You go.) Later we shall see that serious errors may arise from lack of sentence sense.

NOW WORK THE EXERCISE ON PAGE 7

Exercise 2

Trial I IDENTIFY according to MEANING by writing its number in the parentheses (1. declarative; 2. interrogative; 3. imperative; 4. exclamatory):

	Right answers for page 5	Your answers for page 7
1. These are the times that try men's souls.	4	( )
2. Thou, too, sail on, O Ship of State!	5	( )
3. Shall I compare thee to a summer's day?	8	( )
4. He who touches pitch will be defiled.	1	( )
5. Oh! a dainty plant is the ivy green!	3	( )

IDENTIFY according to STRUCTURE (1. simple; 2. compound; 3. complex; 4. compound-complex):

	7	
	2	
	1	
6. The boys and girls shouted and sang.	6	( )
7. When the bugle blows, the troop will advance.	3	( )
8. We crossed the river and then we attacked the enemy.		( )
9. If we study, we shall pass, and then our teacher will be happy.		( )
10. The man dies, but his memory lives.		( )

PLACE S in the parentheses if the italicized word is a simple subject, P if a simple predicate, and N if neither:

	W	
	R	
	W	
11. Then the *lady,* sad and sorry, answered me.	W	( )
12. The moon came over the *mountain.*	R	( )
13. His story *is* a sad one.		( )
14. *There* were many people in the crowd.		( )
15. There we *see* a great man.		( )

CHECK your answers with the right ones on page 9. If all are correct, turn happily to Hints on page 8. If you miss one or more, re-study page 6, and then try Trial II.

Number wrong ____

Trial II IDENTIFY in the manner stated above:
ACCORDING TO MEANING

	5	
1. Blow wind! Come wrack! At least we'll die with harness on our back!	6	( )
2. I am as free as Nature first made man.	1	( )
3. When shall we three meet again?	7	( )
4. Blow, blow, thou Winter Wind!	2	( )
5. Great men only should have great faults.	4	( )

ACCORDING TO STRUCTURE

	1	
	3	
6. A mighty spirit fills that little frame.	8	( )
7. They have sown the wind, and they shall reap the whirlwind.	4	( )
8. Wisdom is often nearest when we stoop.		( )
9. They eat, they drink, and in communion quaff immortality and joy.		( )
10. Man, though dead, retains part of himself.		( )

IDENTIFY subject and predicate in the manner stated above:

	W	
	R	
11. *Shout* and we will come.	W	( )
12. *There* is a lack of interest in this project.	W	( )
13. Today we heard the *news.*	R	( )
14. *John* is the brightest boy in his class.		( )
15. The sexton *told* the story.		( )

CHECK your answers. Use the procedure described on page 5.
AFTER MASTERY, STUDY HINTS ON PAGE 8

Number wrong ____

Hints: Sentence Fragments Grammar

3.0 THE SENTENCE FRAGMENT. We have stressed the importance of the subject and predicate in the sentence. If a group of words does not have a subject and a predicate, expressed or understood, it is a FRAGMENT. Some fragments may be proper, and we give some samples below, but in usual writing do not use unjustifiable sentence fragments. Consider such practice a serious type of error.

Hint 3. Avoid sentence fragments.
A serious error is to use any group of words as if it were a complete sentence.
Wrong: Studying for hours every night.
Right: I was studying for hours every night.
Wrong: Because he called me early.
Right: I went with him because he called me early.
Wrong: He made the team. An athlete of great ability.
Right: He, an athlete of great ability, made the team.

3.1 The dependent clause. The adverbial dependent clause and the adjective dependent clause are frequently used improperly as fragments.
Wrong: I could not afford to go. When suddenly Dad helped me. (Adverbial clause used as fragment)
Right: I could not afford to go. Suddenly Dad helped me. (Dependent clause changed to main clause)
Right: I could not afford to go when suddenly Dad helped me. (Attached fragment to main clause)
Wrong: He awaited her arrival. Which was expected at any time. (Adjective clause)
Right: He awaited her arrival, which was expected at any time. (Attached fragment to main clause)
Right: He awaited her arrival. This was expected at any time. (Changed dependent clause to independent clause)

3.2 The phrase. The phrase may be used improperly as a fragment.
Wrong: After a hard day of work. He often went to a show.
Right: After a hard day of work, he often went to a show. (Attached fragment to the main clause)
Right: After he had worked hard all day, he often went to a show. (Changed phrase to dependent clause)

3.3 Justifiable fragments. According to our idiom, some fragments are justifiable. Here are examples:
Interjections: Pshaw! Indeed!
Greetings: Good-by. Hello.
Transitional statements: But to continue. To summarize.
Elliptical sentences: Never again. My next point.
Skilled writers for stylistic purposes frequently use fragments. We advise that it is not best for you to do so.

NOW WORK THE EXERCISE ON PAGE 9

Exercise 3

Trial I   IDENTIFY by placing in the parentheses an F if the statement is an unjustifiable fragment and an S if it is a proper sentence or a justifiable fragment:

Right answers for page 7 | Your answers for page 9

1. Even the summers which are hot and long. 1 ( )
2. Go! Hurry! Shout! Yell! 3 ( )
3. The task having been accomplished, we hurried home. 2 ( )
4. Sweet are the uses of adversity! 1 ( )
5. She knocked at the door. Hoping no one was home. 4 ( )
6. Whenever the sun rises on a beautiful, refreshing morning. ( )
7. Answer, please. ( )
8. Mr. Brown, who is an excellent tennis player. ( )
9. Early in the morning after he had left us. 1 ( )
10. Smile, and the World smiles with you. 3 ( )
11. No! Never! How absurdly ridiculous! 2 ( )
12. If our cause is right and just. 4 ( )
13. I looked for Jim. First, in his room and then on the campus. 2 ( )
14. I telephoned Jack. My sister's best friend. ( )
15. He always did his duty. ( )

CHECK your answers with the right ones on page 11. If all are correct, turn to page 10 and proceed. If you miss one or more, re-study page 8, and then try

S
N
P
N
P
P

Number wrong

Trial II   IDENTIFY in the same manner as Trial I.

1. Mrs. Smith, who is a friend of the family. ( )
2. The day being cold, we wore overcoats. ( )
3. I came here for a purpose. To see you. ( )
4. Before he visited our beautiful city. ( )
5. Hello! How are you? ( )
6. To succeed, one must work diligently. ( )
7. John entered my room. Then he reported on the game. ( )
8. Being that the car would not start. 4 ( )
9. After tolling the bell. The sexton went home. 1 ( )
10. Because he is the best man on the team. 2 ( )
11. Jack Jones, the flute player, is my chum. 3 ( )
12. Later, the speaker was completely at ease. 1 ( )
13. Never again! I have had enough! ( )
14. That she was a student and studied long hours. ( )
15. She told him to get a job. An idea which pleased him. 1 ( )

2
3
2
3

CHECK your answers as before. If you miss one or more, follow the procedure stated on page 5.

Number wrong

AFTER MASTERY, STUDY HINTS ON PAGE 10

P
N
N
S
P

[9]

Hints: The Comma Splice — Grammar

4.0 THE COMMA SPLICE. The comma is the mark of punctuation showing a small degree of pause. As a mark of separation, the period ranks highest, the semicolon next, and the comma last. The comma is not important enough to substitute for the period or the semicolon in separating independent clauses or sentences.

The comma splice is the error of using a comma between two independent clauses not joined by a coordinating conjunction such as *and, but, or, nor.* The comma splice has earned for itself such ugly names as "comma blunder," "comma fault," or "illiterate comma."

Hint 4. Avoid the comma splice.
The comma splice can be corrected in the following four ways:

4.1 Use the period as the mark of separation.
Wrong: John could not go home for Thanksgiving, he had to work.
Right: John could not go home for Thanksgiving. He had to work.
Wrong: The freshman wrote a theme, it contained many errors.
Right: The freshman wrote a theme. It contained many errors.

4.2 Use the semicolon as the mark of separation.
Wrong: Anxiously I awaited the plane, it was two hours late.
Right: Anxiously I awaited the plane; it was two hours late.
Right: John could not go home for Thanksgiving; he had to work.
Right: The freshman wrote a theme; it contained many errors.

4.3 Use a coordinating conjunction such as *and, but, or, nor,* and retain the comma.
Wrong: The bell rang loud and long, she came into the room.
Right: The bell rang loud and long, and she came into the room.
Wrong: The vacation began on Wednesday, I left Tuesday.
Right: The vacation began on Wednesday, but I left Tuesday.

4.4 Subordinate one of the clauses and retain the comma.
Wrong: My plane began to sputter, it was running out of gas.
Right: My plane began to sputter because it was running out of gas. (Changed one independent clause to a subordinate one)
Right: My plane, running out of gas, began to sputter. (Changed one independent clause into a phrase)
Wrong: The college was small, it had only one hundred freshmen.
Right: The college was small, for it had only one hundred freshmen. (Later we shall give more attention to the proper use of the comma)

NOW WORK EXERCISE ON PAGE 11

Exercise 4

Trial I   SENTENCE ERRORS. In the following there are some fragments and some comma splices. If the sentence is correct, mark R; if a sentence fragment, mark F; if a comma splice, mark CS.

		Right answers for page 9	Your answers for page 11
1.	Oh, what is so rare as a day in June!	F	( )
2.	The whistle blew long and shrill, the man stopped working.	S	( )
3.	Whenever the important course of justice is impeded.	S	( )
4.	She answered me softly and sweetly.	S	( )
5.	She saw the monster. Peeping through the window.	F	( )
6.	They didn't study very much, no one expected them to.	F	( )
7.	He had to work, so he did not go.	S	( )
8.	People like government benefits, but they hate taxes.	F	( )
9.	Seemingly with no place to go.	F	( )
10.	The boys whistled, the girls pretended not to hear.	S	( )
11.	These are the saddest words of tongue or pen.	S	( )
12.	If you could only see the large crowd that applauded.	F	( )
13.	The city has a beautiful golf course, I play there every day.	F	( )
14.	Waving pennants and cheering loudly for the home team.	F	( )
15.	Once to every man and nation comes the moment to decide.	S	( )

CHECK your answers with the right ones on page 13. If all are correct, turn with satisfaction to Hints on page 12. If one or more are incorrect, you know what you should do.

Number wrong ____

Trial II   USE the directions for Trial I.

1.	This is my country.	F	( )
2.	Waving banners and flags and shouting loudly.	S	( )
3.	He wanted to go, he telephoned me.	F	( )
4.	Because he wanted to go, he telephoned me.	F	( )
5.	Not expecting any answer from him.	S	( )
6.	We missed the train, thus we were late.	S	( )
7.	He entered the game; he kicked a goal.	S	( )
8.	Expect us early sometime Friday.	F	( )
9.	After a very long and exciting experience.	F	( )
10.	The engine began to sputter, then it stopped.	F	( )
11.	The class was small, there were only ten members.	S	( )
12.	She is attracting attention. A charming singer.	S	( )
13.	The flowers were blooming beautifully.	S	( )
14.	He is a good worker, let us hire him.	F	( )
15.	He is a good worker. Let us hire him.	F	( )

CHECK your answers as before. If you miss one or more, you know what to do.
AFTER MASTERY, STUDY HINTS ON PAGE 12

Number wrong ____

Hints: The Fused Sentence — Grammar

5.0 THE FUSED SENTENCE. The fused sentence is sometimes called the "Run-together Sentence," or the "Run-on Sentence". It is the serious sentence error in which two sentences have no mark of punctuation between them. It is even worse than the comma splice because the writer using the comma splice recognizes the need of some kind of punctuation, even though he makes the important error of using only the comma.

It will be recalled that a compound sentence consists of two or more main clauses. The Fused Sentence Error usually occurs when the compound sentence consists of two main clauses with no connecting conjunction between them.

Hint 5. Avoid fused sentences.

Do not write two sentences or main clauses without punctuation between them, and this mark should *not* be the comma.

Wrong: I was too tired to study I went home early.
Wrong: The teacher was patient he examined my theme.
Wrong: I was very lonesome when she smiled I spoke to her.

The fused sentence can be corrected in the same four ways used to correct the comma splice:

5.1 Use the period to separate:
Right: I was too tired to study. I went home early.
5.2 Use the semicolon:
Right: The teacher was patient; he examined the theme.
5.3 Use a coordinating conjunction:
Right: I was very lonesome, and, when she smiled, I spoke.
5.4 Use subordination of one main clause:
Right: Because I was too tired to study, I went home early.
Wrong: I went to town the morning sun was shining.
Right: I went to town when the morning sun was shining. (dependent clause)
Right: I went to town in the morning sunshine. (dependent phrase)
5.5 A serious error is to correct a fused sentence by changing it to another error, the comma splice. Instead of the comma, use a more important terminal mark, such as the period, the semicolon, the question mark, or the exclamation point.
Wrong: What shall I do I've lost my wife and seed corn too!
Right: What shall I do! I've lost my wife and seed corn too!

NOW WORK EXERCISE ON PAGE 13

Exercise 5

Trial I If the statement is correct, place R in the proper parentheses; if it is the error known as a fragment, place an F; if a comma splice, place CS; if a fused sentence, place FS.

		Right answers for page 11	Your answers for page 13
1.	I do not care for girls are often fickle.	R	( )
2.	The day was bright and pleasant to take a walk was fun.	CS	( )
3.	He ran for a touchdown, the crowd applauded in glee.	F	( )
4.	Take an umbrella along the clouds indicate rain.	R	( )
5.	John, cheerful and smiling, having finished his dinner.	F	( )
6.	Sweet are the uses of adversity.	CS	( )
7.	Go if you want to stay if you agree with me	CS	( )
8.	If wishes were horses, beggars would ride.	R	( )
9.	The policeman was very polite, he answered me courteously.	F	( )
10.	The man shot the thief ran down the street.	CS	( )
11.	The order has been given, the troops will return home.	R	( )
12.	In spite of all the fury and thunder which we hear.	F	( )
13.	Socrates said that he who might be better employed was idle.	CS	( )
14.	The groves were God's first temples.	F	( )
15.	Having planned and arranged the whole involved performance.	R	( )

CHECK your answers with the right ones on page 15. If all are correct, Comrade, advance! If you miss one or more—Ouch! You know what to do!

Number wrong _____

Trial II FOLLOW the instructions for Trial I.

1.	A jest loses its point when the jester laughs himself.	R	( )
2.	He refused to pay he slammed the door.	F	( )
3.	The man shot the girl screamed.	CS	( )
4.	In an eager attempt at reconciliation.	R	( )
5.	A little learning is a dangerous thing.	F	( )
6.	He called at my home he wished to sell me a book.	CS	( )
7.	Knowing better what to do all along.	R	( )
8.	Ignorance of the law excuses no man.	R	( )
9.	He told me his story; then he asked me for a dollar.	F	( )
10.	During a long and tedious lecture.	CS	( )
11.	Do not insist, I will not go!	CS	( )
12.	The student handed in his paper, he knew he had failed.	F	( )
13.	Whenever the birds sing to me in the morning.	R	( )
14.	Never say die!	CS	( )
15.	We live and learn, why aren't we wiser?	R	( )

CHECK your answers as before.
WHEN YOU ARE SURE OF MASTERY, STUDY HINTS ON PAGE 14

Number wrong _____

Hints: The Complements   Grammar

6.0 OTHER IMPORTANT PARTS OF THE SENTENCE. In addition to the simple subject and simple predicate as previously described, we need to be clear on other important parts of the sentence known as complements: the direct object, the indirect object, the subjective complement, the objective complement, and the object of a preposition.

6.1 THE DIRECT OBJECT receives the action of the verb: He hit the *ball*. He slew a *lion*. She sang a *song*. He wrote a *letter*.
    6.11 A TRANSITIVE VERB requires an object to complete its meaning: *Hit, slew, sang, wrote* are transitive verbs.
    6.12 AN INTRANSITIVE VERB does not require an object: He *ran*. She *sees*. He *was* happy. She *appeared* anxious. It *seems* ripe.

6.2 THE INDIRECT OBJECT names the person to or for whom something is done: I gave *her* a rose. She did *me* a favor. Mother told *Jennie* a story. (If you can put *to* or *for* before the word, it is an *indirect* object, not a direct object)

6.3 THE SUBJECTIVE COMPLEMENT completes the verb and refers to the subject. It may be a noun, pronoun, or adjective.
    Noun: Henry is *king*.
    Pronoun: The lady we mentioned is *she*.
    Adjective: The campus is *green*.
    6.31 THE SUBJECTIVE COMPLEMENT follows forms of the verb *be*, such as *am, is, was, are:* I *am* hungry. He *is* my hero.
    6.32 THE SUBJECTIVE COMPLEMENT follows, also, the verbs of the five senses - look, taste, smell, sound, and feel: I feel *better*. She looks *beautiful*. It tastes *sweet*. It sounds *correct*. It smells *ripe*.
    6.33 The subjective complement follows, also, such linking verbs as *seem, appear, grow, remain, prove:* She seems a clever *person*. She remained *faithful*. It proved *wrong*.

Hint 6. Do not use an adverb as a subjective complement.
Correct usage demands an adjective, and not an adverb.
Wrong: The milk tastes sourly.
Right: The milk tastes sour.
Wrong: The flower smells sweetly.
Right: The flower smells sweet.

6.4 THE OBJECTIVE COMPLEMENT completes the meaning of certain verbs and belongs to the object. Important verbs in this group are *appoint, choose, elect, make:* They appointed John *captain*. The team chose him *leader*. England made Elizabeth *queen*. They elected Mary *president*. (John *to be* captain, him *to be* leader, Elizabeth *to be* queen, Mary *to be* president)

6.5 THE OBJECT OF A PREPOSITION is the important word following the preposition and refers to some other word in the sentence: He went to *town*. The city stood on a *hill*. He climbed over the *fence*. He fell into the *water*. Over the *fence* is out.

NOW WORK EXERCISE ON PAGE 15

Exercise 6

Trial I   IDENTIFY the italicized words by using the proper number (1. subject; 2. direct object; 3. indirect object; 4. The object of a preposition; 5. the subjective complement; 6. the objective complement):

		Right answers for page 13	Your answers for page 15
1.	He went into the *woods*.	FS	( )
2.	The *man* in the car spoke to me	FS	( )
3.	The tree was very *tall*.	CS	( )
4.	They made him *president*.	FS	( )
5.	They gave *her* a beautiful present.	F	( )
6.	The *chairman* called for order.	R	( )
7.	He knocked a *home run*.	FS	( )
8.	Jim is a *sophomore*.	R	( )
9.	The flower smells *sweet*.	CS	( )
10.	They called him *silly*.	FS	( )

In the following statements, mark R if right and W if wrong:

		CS	
		F	
		R	
11.	He felt badly.	R	( )
12.	He swam strongly and swiftly.	F	( )
13.	It looked good to the class.		( )
14.	He arrived safe because he drove safely.		( )
15.	The flute sounds correct.		( )

CHECK your answers with the right ones on page 17. If all are correct, move ahead with pride. If you miss one or more, you know what to do.

Number wrong

Trial II   USE the directions for Trial I:

		R	
		FS	
		FS	
1.	They appointed Jane *secretary*.	F	( )
2.	Jane is now an officer of the *club*.	R	( )
3.	In the town are manufactured many beautiful *articles*.	FS	( )
4.	He tossed the *ball* through the basket.	F	( )
5.	We went toward the big *tree*.	R	( )
6.	She gave *Jane* a box of candy.	R	( )
7.	They named the baby *Josephine*.	F	( )
8.	Lend *me* your ears.	CS	( )
9.	He walked to the center of the *room*.	CS	( )
10.	They were a chosen *people*.	F	( )

Mark R for right; W for wrong:

		R	
		CS	
11.	It tastes sweetly.		( )
12.	He looks sour because he thinks sourly.		( )
13.	The school orchestra sounded beautifully.		( )
14.	He answered correctly.		( )
15.	The metal felt cool.		( )

CHECK your answers as before. Assure yourself of complete mastery.
WHEN YOU ARE SURE OF MASTERY, TURN TO PAGE 16

Number wrong

Review   Grammar

We are now ready to check how well you have mastered the first six exercises.

Review the preceding pages and give special attention whether or not you now understand the corrections of any errors you have previously made.

When you have this assurance, then with confidence TAKE THE REVIEW TEST ON PAGE 17.
GOOD LUCK!

After taking the test, CHECK with the right answers on page 19. Place an X before each item that you miss and record the total wrong in the blank under the test. Then grade yourself by this scale:

	ERRORS	GRADE
	0 - 2	A
	3 - 4	B
	5 - 6	C
	7 - 8	D
More than	8	F, or failed.

If you miss none, or only one, CONGRATULATIONS! You are then ready to advance to page 18.

If you miss three or more, re-study each item missed to the point of complete mastery. Note that we have given you in the Key on page 19 a direct reference to the basic principle of each item on the test. Thus, R-6.1 means the item was right, and the reason is Item 6.1 on page 14. Put oil on every squeak! Do not proceed to page 18 until YOU HAVE MASTERED THE FIRST FIFTEEN PAGES

Review Test I

Review Test I IDENTIFY by appropriate number the italicized word:
 A. PARTS OF SPEECH. (1. noun; 2. pronoun; 3. verb; 4. adjective; 5. adverb; 6. preposition; 7. conjunction; 8. interjection.)

	Right answers for page 15	Your answers for page 17
1. All escaped *save* the captain.	4	( )
2. We shall not see his *like* again.	1	( )
3. His words were low and *sweet*.	5	( )
4. *Neither* Jim *nor* John answered our questions.	6	( )

B. KINDS OF SENTENCES ACCORDING TO MEANING. (9. declarative; 10. interrogative; 11. imperative; 12. exclamatory).

	3	
	1	
	2	
5. Let me go! I will not answer!	5	( )
6. He built a strong and beautiful boat.	5	( )
7. When shall we three meet again?	6	( )

C. KINDS OF SENTENCES ACCORDING TO STRUCTURE. (13. simple; 14. compound; 15. complex; 16. compound-complex).

8. Whenever Duty calls, Youth answers.	W	( )
9. He bought a beautiful pony, and then he placed on it an expensive saddle of richest leather.	R R	( )
10. Little pigs squeal for milk, but hogs grunt and eat whatever is put before them.	R R R	( )

D. PARTS OF SENTENCES. (17. direct object; 18. subjective complement; 19. indirect object; 20. objective complement; 21. object of a preposition).

11. She is a gentle and attractive *lady*.		( )
12. We made him our *commander*.		( )
13. She gave *him* an order.		( )
14. The letter is on top of the *file*.	6	( )
15. The next day the grass looked fresh and *green*.	4	( )

E. CORRECTIONS. In the following statements, mark R if correct, and W if wrong:

	1	
	2	
	4	
16. He sure swam good.	3	( )
17. After having made this long and powerful speech.	6	( )
18. All's well that ends well.	3	( )
19. He knocked at my door at midnight, I got up and answered it.	4	( )
20. All went except he and I.	5	( )
21. Brutus is an honorable man.		( )
22. I went for the doctor was not in his office.		( )
23. After this great task had been accomplished.		( )
24. It tastes bitterly.	W	( )
25. Strive to arrive alive!	R	( )
26. This cigarette tastes like it should.	W	( )
27. He crossed the river safely, and all are pleased to hear that he is safe.	R	( )
28. He opened the door. Because the bell had been ringing a long time.	R	( )
29. She answered sourly, "It tastes sour!"		( )
30. Let us go with him!		( )

Number wrong _____

Grade _____

[17]

Hints: Nouns and Number — Grammar

7.0 THE NOUN. The noun is a basic part of speech. It is the symbol for an idea. It is the name of a person, place, or thing. Sometimes it names an action or a quality.

7.1 A common noun names a member of a class: The *man* came. *White* is pretty. The *city* is large. The *sky* is blue. Common nouns may be *collective, concrete,* or *abstract*.

7.2 A collective noun names a group: *family; crew; flock; team; committee; class.*

7.3 A concrete noun names something that can be perceived by the senses: *house; tree; star; table; ceiling.*

7.4 An abstract noun names an idea or a quality: *purity; whiteness; integrity; strength; kindness.*

7.5 A proper noun names something specific, usually the only one of its class. It is capitalized: *Ohio; Lincoln;* the *Hesperus; Christmas; England.*

7.6 Nouns have number, gender, and case.
    7.61 Number indicates whether or not the word is singular (one) or plural (more than one).
    7.62 Gender indicates sex—male, female, or neuter.
    7.63 Case indicates relationships in the sentence—nominative, possessive, or objective. Gender and case will be given more attention later.

Hint 7. Make your subject agree in number with its verb.
Both verb and subject should be plural, or both verb and subject should be singular. Do not use the singular form of a noun for the plural, or the plural form for the singular.
    Wrong: He walked two mile (two *miles*).
    Wrong: The data is correct (*are* correct).

7.71 Most nouns form the plural by adding s to the singular: car, *cars;* girl, *girls;* dog, *dogs;* tree, *trees.*

7.72 Nouns ending in an *s* sound form the plural by adding *es* and pronouncing this ending as an extra syllable: box, *boxes;* church, *churches;* tax, *taxes;* bush, *bushes.*

7.8 A collective noun takes a singular verb when the group is thought of as a unit and a plural verb when the members of the group are emphasized:
    Unit: The committee *meets* tonight.
    Members: The committee *are* disagreeing among themselves.

7.9 English has taken its nouns from many languages with varying rules for forming the plural: chief, *chiefs;* loaf, *loaves;* alumnus, *alumni;* datum; *data;* child, *children.*

Hint 8. Check all doubtful plurals by use of the dictionary.

NOW WORK THE EXERCISE ON PAGE 19 (Use your dictionary when in doubt)

Exercise 7

	Right answers for page 17	Your answers for page 19

Trial I   CLASSIFY by number the italicized words (1. proper noun; 2. common noun):

	Right answers for page 17	Your answers for page 19
1. *Mother* gave me this ring.	6–1.6	( )
2. Respect should be paid to every *mother*.	1–1.1	( )
3. Every class has its *president*.	4–1.4	( )
4. Gentlemen, here is the *President* of the United States.	7–1.7	( )
5. *Alaska* is now a state.		( )

CLASSIFY by number the italicized words (3. a collective noun; 4. an abstract noun; 5. a concrete noun):

	12–2.54	
6. Truth and *Beauty* are rare attributes.	9–2.51	( )
7. The *rose* was a dark red.	10–2.52	( )
8. The lowing *herd* winds slowly o'er the lea.		( )
9. *Honesty* and valor belong to the true gentleman.		( )

PLACE R if right; W if wrong:

	15–2.63	
10. The fairys were dainty and beautiful.		( )
11. This phenomena is unusual.	14–2.62	( )
12. Due respect should be paid to mothers-in-law.		( )
13. The team were unable to elect a captain.	16–2.64	( )
14. The team carries out its signals well.		( )
15. The wages of sin is death.		( )

CHECK your answers with the right ones on page 21. If you miss one or more, try Trial II. After mastery, go to page 20.

	18–6.31	Number wrong
	20–6.4	

Trial II   CLASSIFY proper and common nouns as in Trial I:

	19–6.2	
	21–6.5	
1. The *Amazon* is a long river.	18–6.32	( )
2. He crossed a *river*.		( )
3. *Father* always tried to be a good father.		( )
4. He was the best *father* in the world.		( )
5. With a dirty *coin* I bought a rose.		( )

CLASSIFY collective, abstract, and concrete nouns as in Trial I:

	W–1.5	
	W–3.2	
	R–2.51	
6. The *rain* fell in torrents.	W–4.0	( )
7. These three are faith, hope, and *charity*.	W–1.6	( )
8. The *crew* won a victory.	R–2.51	( )
9. I heard the *echo*.	W–5.2	( )

PLACE R if right; W, if wrong:

	W–3.1	
	W–6.32	
10. The chimnies were smoking.	R–2.53	( )
11. The data are before you.	W–1.6	( )
12. The team are fighting with each other.	R–2.64	( )
13. The vallies are very deep and wide.	W–3.1	( )
14. We have too many mouses in our house!	R–6.32	( )
15. He bought two loafs of bread.	R–2.53	( )

CHECK your answers as before. When you are sure of MASTERY, TURN TO PAGE 20

Number wrong

[19]

Hints: The Pronoun Grammar

9.0 A pronoun substitutes for a noun or another pronoun. The noun it substitutes for is called the *antecedent* of the pronoun. The use of the pronoun avoids repetition and monotony. Here are some pronouns: *He* saw the gun *which he* had given *him*. *She* liked *him* because of *his* enthusiasm.

9.1 There are eight kinds of pronouns, and they may be used grammatically in the same way as nouns. Here is the list: personal, relative, demonstrative, interrogative, reflexive, intensive, indefinite, and reciprocal.

9.2 A personal pronoun refers to a person or persons: *I, you, he*. *I* is in the first person—the speaker; *you*, in the second person—the one spoken to; *he*, in the third person—the one spoken about. The personal pronoun is difficult because it has more case forms than the other pronouns. Note the following:

DECLENSION OF THE PERSONAL PRONOUN

Number	Person	Nominative Case	Possessive Case	Objective Case
Singular	First	I	my, mine	me
	Second	you	your, yours	you
	Third	he	his	him
		she	her, hers	her
		it	its	it
Plural	First	we	our, ours	us
	Second	you	your, yours	you
	Third	they	their, theirs	them

9.3 A relative pronoun introduces a clause: *who, which, whom, whose, that*. This is the house *that* Jack built.

9.4 A demonstrative pronoun points out: *this, that, these, those, such*. *Such* is our case.

9.5 An interrogative pronoun introduces a question: *who, which, what, whose, whom*. *Whose* is that?

9.6 A reflexive pronoun directs its action back to the subject: *myself, yourself, himself, themselves*. I hurt *myself*.

Hint 9. Do not use a reflexive pronoun as a personal pronoun.
    Wrong: Mary and *myself* attended (Mary and *I*).
    He gave both John and *myself* a program (John and *me*).

9.7 An intensive pronoun has the form of a reflexive pronoun and is used for emphasis: He *himself* said he would act. The freshmen *themselves* reported the story. She *herself* answered the phone.

9.8 An indefinite pronoun does not refer to a particular person: *Someone* did it. *Nobody* cares. *Few* recall the incident. *Each* replied. *Everybody* shouted. *Anyone* could do it.

9.9 A reciprocal pronoun indicates an interchange of action. There are two: *one another* and *each other*.
    They threw the ball to *one another* (more than two).
    They gave gifts to *each other* (two only).

NOW WORK THE EXERCISE ON PAGE 21

Exercise 8

Trial I   CLASSIFY by number the italicized pronouns (1. personal; 2. relative; 3. demonstrative; 4. interrogative; 5. reflexive; 6. intensive; 7. indefinite; 8. reciprocal):

		Right answers for page 19	Your answers for page 21
1.	The general said, "*I* will try."	1	( )
2.	*Who* is the boss here?	2	( )
3.	*Everybody* likes to watch television.	2	( )
4.	He *himself* should assume authority.	1	( )
5.	The two boys shouted to *each other*.	1	( )
6.	*This* is the bat I want.		( )
7.	The girl *who* won is my sister.		( )
8.	He showed *himself* that he could.		( )

Place R if right; W, if wrong:

		4	
		5	
		3	
9.	John and myself attended the game.	4	( )
10.	He shot himself.		( )
11.	The group argued among themselves.		( )
12.	He answered that one hisself.	W	( )
13.	As for myself, count me out.	W	( )
14.	It was her who did the damage.	R	( )
15.	The three girls discussed roommates with one another.	R	( )
		R	
		R	

CHECK your answers with the right ones on page 23. If you miss one or more, try

_____
Number wrong

Trial II   CLASSIFY as in Trial I:

1.	My wife said that *she* would do it.		( )
2.	*Who* owns that cottage?	1	( )
3.	This is the boy *who* raised his hand.	2	( )
4.	She promised *herself* a test.	1	( )
5.	*Anyone* could do better.	2	( )
6.	*Those* are the sounds I mentioned.	2	( )
7.	She *herself* answered the bell.		( )
8.	The two men assisted *each other*.		( )

Place R if right; W, if wrong.

		5	
		4	
		3	
9.	The project did not reach it's goal.	5	( )
10.	He and myself went hunting.		( )
11.	I myself will answer that letter.		( )
12.	Which novel do you recommend?		( )
13.	As for myself, I prefer the high road.	W	( )
14.	He hurt hisself in the gym.	R	( )
15.	The seniors themselves had this honor.	R	( )
		W	
		W	
		W	

CHECK the right answers on page 23. When mastery is complete, **TURN TO PAGE 22**

_____
Number wrong

[21]

Hints: Pronouns and Antecedents Grammar

10.0 The antecedent is the noun or pronoun for which the pronoun stands. The pronoun has the same number, gender, and person as the antecedent. Thus it is said that a pronoun agrees with its antecedent in these three respects. Its case depends on its relationship with other words in the sentence.

Hint 10. See that a pronoun agrees with its antecedent in number.

10.1 If the antecedent is singular, the pronoun should be singular; if the antecedent is plural, the pronoun should be plural.
   Singular: The player did *his* best.
   Plural: The players did *their* best.

10.2 Two or more antecedents joined by *and* (or any other coordinating conjunction) take a plural pronoun: Mary and Alice paid *their* dues.

10.3 Singular antecedents joined by *or* or *nor* take a singular pronoun: Neither Mary nor Alice paid *her* dues.

10.4 If one antecedent is singular and the other is plural, the pronoun agrees with the nearer antecedent:
   Neither the captain nor the players *know* their signals.
   Neither the players nor the captain *knows* their signals.

10.5 A collective noun takes a singular or a plural pronoun depending whether the meaning is the unit as a whole or the parts of the unit.
   Whole: The team played *its* best. (As a unit)
   Parts: The team disagreed among *themselves*. (Parts of the unit)

10.6· The following indefinite pronouns are singular: *another, anybody, anyone, each, either, everybody, neither, nobody, no one, some one.*
   Wrong: Each did *their* best (*his* best).
   Wrong: Neither acted *their* part well (*his* part).
   Wrong: Everybody sent *their* gift (*his* gift).

10.7 An appositive is a noun or pronoun added to another noun or pronoun to explain it. This appositive agrees in number, gender, person, and case with this noun or pronoun.
   Poe, an American *author,* wrote "The Raven."

Hint 11. See that a demonstrative pronoun used as an adjective agrees in number with the noun which it modifies.
It will be recalled that the demonstrative pronouns are *this, that, these, those,* and *such.* When used to modify nouns they are adjectives.
   Wrong: I like *those* kind of apples.
   Right: I like *that* kind of apples.
   Right: I like *those kinds* of apples.
   Right: He admires *this* type of athletes (not *these type*).
   Right: He enjoys *those kinds* of plays (not *those kind*).

NOW WORK EXERCISE ON PAGE 23

Exercise 9

		Right answers for page 21	Your answers for page 23

Trial I   PLACE R if right; W, if wrong:

1. The committee has elected its chairman.   1   ( )
2. The committee are considering their ballots.   4   ( )
3. I hate those kind of players.   7   ( )
4. Everyone did their best.   6   ( )
5. The tree is tall and mighty.   8   ( )
6. Neither Jim nor Jack answers his mail.   3   ( )
7. Jim and Jack are good friends.   2   ( )
8. Everybody sent their best wishes.   5   ( )
9. Either Joe or Dick returned their tickets.   ( )
10. Harry, Ralph, and Elsa gave their share.   ( )
11. Neither the teacher nor the pupils honor the flag.   ( )
12. The congregation fought among themselves.   W   ( )
13. He praises those kind of answers.   R   ( )
14. England expects each man to do his duty.   R   ( )
15. Jones, our best guard, broke his ankle.   W   ( )

CHECK your answers with the right ones on page 25. If you miss one or more, try   W
Trial II. After mastery, go to page 24.   W
                                                                                     R   Number
                                                                                             wrong

Trial II   Mark as in Trial I:

1. Neither sent their gift.   ( )
2. I like them kind of pears.   ( )
3. Whittier, a Quaker, wrote *Snow Bound*.   1   ( )
4. Mary and I plan to go.   4   ( )
5. Neither the team nor the coach knows the answers.   2   ( )
6. An apple a day drives the doctor away.   5   ( )
7. The committee adjourned their meeting.   7   ( )
8. Nobody did his best.   3   ( )
9. I like this type of friends.   6   ( )
10. Neither Jack nor Joe return their books.   8   ( )
11. Either Ann or Mary will rejoin her class.   ( )
12. Neither the teacher nor the pupils encourage their friends.   ( )
13. Neither the pupils nor the teacher encourages her friends.   ( )
14. I approve those kind of efforts.   W   ( )
15. I am the captain of this ship.   W   ( )

CHECK the right answers on page 25. After mastery,   R
TURN TO PAGE 24   R
                                                         W   Number
                                                         W   wrong
                                                         R

[23]

Hints: Antecedent Problems — Grammar

12.0 The pronoun generally refers to the nearest antecedent (This is known as the Law of Proximity); but sometimes a remote emphatic, prominent noun steals the reference (This is known as the Law of Prominence). Then we must change to get clarity.
- Wrong: The commander told the man that he would go. (Is *commander* or *man* the antecedent?)
- Right: The commander told the man, "You may go."

Hint 12. When either of two words may be the antecedent for a pronoun, reword so the antecedent is clear.
- Wrong: The doctor told the clerk that he should call.
- Right: The doctor said to the clerk, "I shall call."

Hint 13. Avoid using clauses, sentences, or vague references as antecedents.
- Wrong: He knocked a home-run. *This* excited the crowd.
- Right: He knocked a home-run. *This act* excited the crowd.
- Wrong: I forgot your address, *which* is the cause for my delay.
- Right: I forgot your address, *which fact* is the cause for my delay.

Hint 14. Avoid forming illiterate reflexive or intensive pronouns.
- Wrong: He hurt *hisself* (for *himself*).
  - The tool *itsself* is sharp (for *itself*).
  - Said I to *meself*, "Let's go!" (for *myself*)

Hint 15. Use the relative pronoun *who* with persons, *which* with things, and *that* with persons or things.
- Wrong: The swan, *who* swam gracefully, disappeared (*which*).
  - The boy *which* answered you is my son (*who* or *that*)

Hint 16. Avoid repeating a personal pronoun directly after its antecedent.
- Wrong: My friend *he* answered the bell. (Omit *he*)
  - Our music teacher *she* asked me to sing. (Omit *she*)

Hint 17. Avoid overworking *it, you, they* as the subject of a sentence.
- Poor: It showed in this book the importance of hard work.
- Better: This book showed the importance of hard work.
- Poor: They have good football teams in the Big Ten.
- Better: The Big Ten has good football teams.

Hint 18. Avoid overworking *I*, and in a series of references to persons, use *I* last for the sake of courtesy.
- Exception: In a matter of blame or fault, place *I* first.
- Right: I and the others are to blame.
- Wrong: *I* and Mom washed the dishes (Mom and *I*).
  - *I* and he won the match (He and *I*).
  - *I*, James, and Bob went to the show (James, Bob, and *I*)

WORK THE EXERCISE ON PAGE 25

Exercise 10

	Right answers for page 23	Your answers for page 25

Trial I   PLACE R if right; W, if wrong:

1. I and Betty killed a bear! — R ( )
2. In this accident he hurt hisself. — R ( )
3. He said those truths could be verified. — W ( )
4. This is the house that Jack built. — W ( )
5. My girl she gave me a book for Christmas. — R ( )
6. He slapped me on the face, which is my cause for anger. — R ( )
7. My teacher he works me day after day. — R ( )
8. The teacher told the pupil that he worked too hard. — W ( )
9. You can read in the book how to work puzzles. — W ( )
10. I praised him publicly. This act made him my friend. — R ( )
11. The chairman which you addressed answered you. — R ( )
12. Our dog, who sleeps in my study, barked at him. — R ( )
13. I, Jim, and Jane each gave a quarter. — W ( )
14. The teacher told John that John should study more. — R ( )
15. He said to hisself, "That's enough!" — R ( )

CHECK your answers with the right ones on page 27. Advance if you have missed none. If you have missed one or more, try

Number wrong _____

Trial II   Place R if right; W, if wrong:

1. The hook itsself is dull. — W ( )
2. The storekeeper told the clerk that he was tired. — W ( )
3. I and you make a good team! — R ( )
4. Is it true that all men are created equal? — R ( )
5. I know in whom I have confidence. — R ( )
6. He fumbled the ball, which lost us the game. — R ( )
7. Says I to meself, "Don't be scared!" — W ( )
8. They serve good food, the Triangle Restaurant does. — R ( )
9. My teacher, he always abuses me. — R ( )
10. Jane, Judy, and I attended the game. — W ( )
11. This is the story that he told me. — R ( )
12. That animal who bit me ran away. — R ( )
13. The policeman knew that he would not do what he said. — R ( )
14. Do what is best. — W ( )
15. These exercises, they seem too easy! — R ( )

AFTER MASTERY, TURN TO PAGE 26

Number wrong _____

[25]

Nominative
Hints: Case of Nouns and Pronouns and Objective

19.0   Case in a noun or pronoun shows its relationship to other words in a sentence. A word is said to be inflected if it changes its form to show its case. English does not have as many cases as do other languages and fewer inflections. In fact, it has only three cases—nominative, possessive (genitive), and objective (accusative). Pronouns have more inflections than nouns. Review the table of the declension of personal pronouns as given on page 20. We decline a word when we name all the case forms it has. Most of our grammatical problems arise because pronouns may have different forms for the different cases.

Hint 19. Place all nouns and pronouns in their proper case.

19.1   Nouns and pronouns used as subjects or subjective complements are in the nominative case.
         Wrong: John and *me* bought a boat (John and *I*).
                 It was *them* that made the decision (*they*).
                 It was *him* (*he*). It was *me* (*I*). It was *her* (*she*).
Him, me, her in these examples are accepted by some grammarians on the basis of the frequency of their usage, but many careful speakers and writers still prefer It is *he;* it was *I;* it was *she*.

19.2   The object of a verb or a preposition is in the objective case.
         Wrong: The teacher praised Jim and *I (me)*.
                He did it for you and *I (me)*.
Except and *but* may be used as prepositions and then take the objective case: None came but *him*. None went except *him*.

19.3   The indirect object of a verb is in the objective case.
         Right: Write *him* a letter. Give *me* the book. Send *her* a gift.

19.4   The subject of an infinitive, the object of an infinitive, the objective complement of an infinitive is each in the objective case. An infinitive is a verbal generally preceded by *to,* expressed or implied. It will be discussed later in more detail.
         Examples: They asked *him* to answer it. They made him (to) do it. Did you take *her* to be *him?*
     Whom did you take him to be?

19.5   The case of a relative pronoun is determined by its use in a sentence. The correct use of *who* and *whom* is the most serious problem. When in doubt, try substituting *he* or *him*. If *he* is right, so is *who;* if *him* is right, so is *whom:*
         Wrong: Who are you speaking to (to he or to him?)?
         Right: Whom are you speaking to?
         Wrong: He is the kind of athlete *who* we want (we want *he* or *him?*)
         Right: He is the kind of athlete *whom* we want.

19.6   An appositive should be in the same case as the word it explains:
         Wrong: He advised both of us, Jack and *I (me)*.
                The singers, Jane and *me,* sang our number *(I)*.

WORK THE EXERCISE ON PAGE 27

Exercise 11

		Right answers for page 25	Your answers for page 27
Trial I	Place R if right; W, if wrong:		
1.	Who are you waiting for?	W	( )
2.	To whom will you give this gift?	W	( )
3.	The teacher asked you and I to wait after school.	R	( )
4.	He called for you and me.	R	( )
5.	It was she who answered the phone.	W	( )
6.	Both of us students, Jack and me, do our best.	W	( )
7.	It was they who stole the car.	W	( )
8.	Is there one whom you detest?	W	( )
9.	Is it him who you called?	W	( )
10.	The captain praised Jim, Jerry, and I.	R	( )

INDICATE case of italicized word by writing *N* if nominative and *O* if objective:

		W	
		W	
		W	
11.	She is the *owner* of the car.	R	( )
12.	Write *him* a letter.	W	( )
13.	He urged *him* to try again.		( )
14.	Washington, our first *president*, worked long hours.		( )
15.	All came to the party except *Jim*.		( )

CHECK your answers with the right ones on page 29. Go ahead if you have missed none. If you have missed one or more, try

Number wrong

		W	
Trial II	Place R if right; W, if wrong:	W	
		W	
1.	Now, as far as you and me are concerned, I agree.	R	( )
2.	Mother asked you and me to clean the kitchen.	R	( )
3.	The teacher praised John, Mary, and I.	W	( )
4.	Who are you calling for?	W	( )
5.	Both of we players did our best.	W	( )
6.	All did the work except him.	W	( )
7.	Is it her you are after?	R	( )
8.	The coach praised Jim and I.	R	( )
9.	She did it for her and me.	W	( )
10.	All went but him.	W	( )
		R	
		W	

INDICATE case of italicized words by writing N for nominative and O for objective:

11.	He is the ruler of the *country*.		( )
12.	Dickens, a famous *novelist*, wrote that book.		( )
13.	To hold this fort remained only the *men*.		( )
14.	They wanted him to be called *Luke*.		( )
15.	They sentenced *him* to death.		( )

AFTER MASTERY, TURN TO PAGE 28.

Number wrong

Hints: The Possessive Case — Grammar

20.0 The possessive case, sometimes called the genitive case, in its simplest use shows ownership or possession. On page 20 you can see the various forms the pronoun assumes in this case. Nouns usually use the apostrophe to form the possessive case.

Hint 20. Build possessive cases correctly and precisely.

20.1 Use an apostrophe and *s* to form the possessive case of a noun not ending in *s*.
    Example: Mr. Smith's office is on the second floor.

20.2 Add the apostrophe alone to form the possessive case of a plural noun ending in *s*.
    Example: The girls' gym is new and well-equipped.

20.3 Also, to form the possessive, add the apostrophe alone to nouns ending in *s* if an added *s* would make pronunciation awkward or difficult.
    Example: Socrates' dialogues; for goodness' sake; Moses' law.

20.4 Add an apostrophe and *s* to form the possessive case of the indefinite pronouns: anybody's; somebody else's; another's. But do not use the apostrophe and *s* with the personal pronouns: his; her; its; ours, yours, theirs. A common mistake is to use *it's* as the possessive case of *it*. It's is the abbreviation for *it is*. Wrong: You know it's direction (its).

20.5 Avoid an awkward use of the possessive case; use an *of* phrase instead.
    Wrong: The *barn's* roof leaked (roof of the barn).
             The *tree's* leaves were brown (leaves of the tree).
             We ate dinner at one of the *girls'* home (at the home of one of the girls).

20.6 Use the possessive case to express time or measurement: a day's work; a moment's notice; a stone's throw; a yard's length.

20.7 Use the possessive case with objects which have been personified: the Ocean's roar; Nature's laws; the Mountain's majesty.

20.8 A noun or pronoun linked with a gerund should be in the possessive case. (A gerund is a verbal noun, and will be described later in more detail.)
    Wrong: We liked him singing ballads.
             We liked *his singing* ballads.
    Wrong: She objected to the girl belonging to that sorority.
             She objected to the *girl's belonging* to that sorority.

NOW WORK EXERCISE ON PAGE 29

Exercise 12

	Right answers for page 27	Your answers for page 29

Trial I   Place R if right; W, if wrong:

1. They painted the boys' dormitory. — W ( )
2. He called for it's destruction. — R ( )
3. This is mine and that is his'n. — W ( )
4. It's proper to salute the flag. — R ( )
5. He likes to read Dickens' works. — R ( )
6. He bought ten cent's worth of candy. — W ( )
7. Mens' hats are on sale now. — R ( )
8. The house's windows need repair. — R ( )
9. We knew of him robbing the orchard. — W ( )
10. The responsibility is all their's. — W ( )
11. It's time for its departure. — ( )
12. This is Lewis' new car. — ( )
13. The sad Sea's whispering quieted me. — ( )
14. His is her'n and her'n is his'n! — N ( )
15. He looked at the automobile's paint. — O ( )

N
O
CHECK your answers with the right ones on page 31. Go ahead if you have   N   Number
missed none. If you have missed one or more, try   O   wrong

Trial II   Place R if right; W, if wrong:

1. The roof's leaking was serious. — ( )
2. The Prairie's call enticed him. — ( )
3. They visited the womens' prison. — ( )
4. He spoke in behalf of it's cause. — W ( )
5. Them always belonged to us'n! — R ( )
6. It's always right to defend the right. — W ( )
7. We enjoy his reciting poetry. — W ( )
8. Some were her'n and his'n and some were mine and you'n! — W ( )
9. It's all in a day's work. — R ( )
10. The credit is all her's. — W ( )
11. He likes to read Demosthenes' speeches. — W ( )
12. He found the childrens' playthings. — R ( )
13. This is anybody's business. — R ( )
14. The Hurricane's fury wrecked his home. — ( )
15. The players' suits were cleaned. — ( )

AFTER MASTERY, TURN TO PAGE 30   Number
                                                                                                                     wrong
O
N
N
O
O

Review • Grammar

Are you ready for the test on the next page?

If you care to, review all errors or difficulties since the last test.

Grade yourself on your first attempt, using the scale set up on page 16. You will recall this is the scale:

ERRORS	GRADE
0 - 2	A
3 - 4	B
5 - 6	C
7 - 8	D
More than 8	F, or failed.

You are making good progress if you make less than three errors on this test. If - and I do so hope you will not! - you make three or more, review till you are sure of mastery.

Note the right answers in the Key on page 33 and references to the Hint for each item missed.

NOW DO THE TEST ON PAGE 31
(And again-Good luck!)

Review Test II

Review Test II — IDENTIFY by appropriate number the italicized words (1. personal pronoun; 2. relative pronoun, 3. demonstrative pronoun; 4. interrogative pronoun; 5. reflexive pronoun; 6. intensive pronoun; 7. indefinite pronoun; 8. reciprocal pronoun.):

Right answers for page 29 | Your answers for page 31

1. He gave *me* the book. — R ( )
2. N*obody* cares. — W ( )
3. They threw the ball to *one another*. — W ( )
4. He *himself* said he would act. — R ( )

IDENTIFY by appropriate number these italicized words (9. appositive; 10. subject of an infinitive; 11. antecedent; 12. direct object; 13. indirect object):

R
W
W
W
W

5. The teacher asked *John* to go. — W ( )
6. She gave *him* a dollar. — R ( )
7. Caesar, our brave *leader,* advanced. — R ( )
8. John asked me and then I answered *him*. — R ( )
9. Please hand *me* my hat. — W ( )

W

IDENTIFY in the same manner (14. nominative case; 15. possessive case; 16. objective case):

10. We tried to make him *president*. — ( )
11. Caesar is our great *leader*. — ( )
12. They denied *Moses'* petition. — ( )
13. We loved *his* reciting. — W ( )
14. They told *him* to reply. — R ( )
15. Elizabeth is our gracious *queen*. — W ( )

W
W
R

Place R if right; W, if wrong:

16. We liked his singing ballads. — R ( )
17. The Ocean's roar deepened as we approached. — W ( )
18. None came but him. — R ( )
19. Neither the captain nor the players knew their signals. — W ( )
20. The team disagreed among themselves. — R ( )
21. You know it's direction. — W ( )
22. He advised both of us, Jack and I. — R ( )
23. Says I to meself, "Let's go!" — R ( )
24. Was it him? — R ( )
25. None came but him. — ( )
26. Who are you speaking to? — ( )
27. My friend, he answered the call. — ( )
28. I and the others are to blame. — ( )
29. The vallies are wide and deep. — ( )
30. The doctor told the clerk that he should call. — ( )

AFTER MASTERY, TURN TO PAGE 32

Number wrong _____

Grade _____

[31]

Hints: Verbs, Linking and Auxiliary Grammar

21.0 Verbs. As previously stated, a verb expresses action or state of being. Every sentence must have a subject, expressed or understood. We have discussed the active verbs, which may be transitive or intransitive (See 6.11 and 6.12). Now we shall give attention to inactive verbs known as *linking verbs* (sometimes called copulative verbs).

21.1 A linking verb joins a subject with a subjective complement.
   Examples: He *is* an athlete. The rose *smells* sweet.

21.2 The most common linking verb is *be* in any of its various forms, such as *am, are, is, was, were*.
   Examples: You *are* the leader. They *were* the pupils.

21.3 Other common linking verbs are those pertaining to the senses: *look, taste, smell, sound, feel*.
   Examples: It *looks* ripe. It *tastes* sweet. It *smells* rotten.

21.4 Other common linking verbs are *appear, become, grow, remain, prove, turn*.
   Examples: It *proved* wrong. He *turned* traitor.

Hint 21. Do not use an adverb to complete a linking verb.
The active verb usually takes an adverb; the linking verb a noun, pronoun, or adjective. Sometimes an active verb may be used also as a linking verb. If this is the case, when it is used as an active verb, use the **adverb**; when it is used as a linking verb, use the adjective.
   Right: He landed *safe* because he landed *safely*.
   The rose smelled *sweet*, and the dainty lady smelled it *sweetly*.
   As he looked *steadily*, he saw the stream looked *muddy*.
   Wrong: It sounds *loudly* (loud). It tastes *sweetly* (sweet).

22.0 Auxiliary verbs are verbs used with other verbs to show tense, mood, and voice. *Auxiliary* is derived from a Latin word meaning *help*, and an auxiliary verb is a helping verb. In the sentence, He did send it home, *did* is an auxiliary verb with *send*.

22.1 Common auxiliary verbs are forms of the verbs *to be, to have, to do*. Other common auxiliaries are *shall, should, will, would, may, might, can, could, must, ought, let, need, used,* and *dare*.
   Examples: He *has* seen the play. It *will* be sent later. You *need* not apply. I *did* reply. I *shall* call on him.

Hint 22. Never use *of* in the place of the auxiliary *have*.
   Wrong: You should *of* done better (have)
   If you had asked, I would *of* gone (have).
   It could *of* been better (have).

22.2 Repeat the auxiliary if clearness demands it.
   Wrong: She does earn a good wage, but spends foolishly.
   Right: She does earn a good wage, but she does spend it foolishly.

NOW WORK EXERCISE 13.

Exercise 13

Trial I   INDICATE type of italicized verb by placing in the parentheses an A if an active verb, an L if a linking verb, and an H if an auxiliary verb:

		Right answers for page 31	Your answers for page 33
1.	Pouring oil on the sea *makes* it calm.	1–9.2	( )
2.	I *should have* done much better.	7–9.8	( )
3.	The rose *smells* sweet.	8–9.9	( )
4.	He *remained* a Republican.	6–9.7	( )

Place R if right; W, if wrong:

5.	It looked good to me.		( )
6.	If I had known, I would of gone.		( )
7.	The rumor proved false.	10–19.4	( )
8.	She does write beautifully but wrote seldom.	13–19.3	( )
9.	He looked suspiciously at the contrivance.	9–19.6	( )
10.	He might of called earlier.	12–19.2	( )
11.	He grew tall.	13–19.3	( )
12.	He looked eagerly for the signal.		( )
13.	The victim was me.		( )
14.	The candy tasted well.		( )
15.	He is well again.		( )

16–19.4	
14–19.1	Number wrong
15–20.3	

CHECK your answers with the right ones on page 35. Go ahead if you have missed none. If you have missed one or more, try

15–20.8
16–19.4
14–19.1

Trial II   DESIGNATE italicized word as indicated above.

1.	The pear *tastes* sweet.	R–20.8	( )
2.	He *called* the man a rascal.	R–20.7	( )
3.	It *should have been* dropped long ago.	R–19.2	( )
4.	The play *appeared* novel and interesting.	R–10.4	( )

R–10.5
W–20.4
W–19.6

Place R if right; W, if wrong:

5.	I should of known better.	W–14.0	( )
6.	He didn't do so good.	W–19.1	( )
7.	He walked slowly down the lane.	R–19.2	( )
8.	He did it by the light of the moon.	W–19.2	( )
9.	Drive careful so you arrive safely.	W–16	( )
10.	This truth remains eternal.	R–18	( )
11.	This cake tastes sweetly.	W–7.72	( )
12.	If he only would of asked me!	W–12.0	( )
13.	She does not play well but tries.		( )
14.	There's a sound of music in the air.		( )
15.	This fur feels roughly.		( )

AFTER MASTERY, TURN TO PAGE 34

Number wrong

Hints: Principal Parts of Verbs — Grammar

23.0 The three principal parts of verbs are the present tense (or the present infinitive), the past tense, and the past participle.

23.1 Most English verbs form the past tense and past participle by adding *d, ed,* or *t* to the present infinitive: walk, walked. These are called *regular* or *weak* verbs, and they cause us little trouble.

23.2 Approximately four hundred verbs form their principal parts irregularly. These cause us difficulty. They are called *irregular* or *strong* verbs, and are among the most common and important in our everyday use. Many of them are very old in the history of our language. No rule for their formation covers all of them. Learn the most important by heart, and when in doubt about the others look them up in your dictionary.

23.3 The present participle is formed by adding *ing* to the present infinitive: give, *giving;* run, *running;* eat, *eating.*

23.4 Here is a list of fifty of these difficult verbs. In sequence you have the present tense (or present infinitive), the past tense, and the past participle:

1. awake, awoke, awaked; 2. be, was, been; 3. bear (carry), bore, borne; 4. bear (birth), bore, born; 5. bid (order), bade, bidden; 6. Blow, blew, blown; 7. burst, burst, burst; 8. Choose, chose, chosen; 9. come, came, come; 10. do, did, done; 11. draw, drew, drawn; 12. drink, drank, drunk; 13. drive, drove, driven; 14. eat, ate, eaten; 15. fall, fell, fallen; 16. give, gave, given; 17. go, went, gone; 18. hang (object), hung, hung; 19. hang (person), hanged, hanged; 20. have, had, had; 21. hide, hid, hidden; 22. lay (transitive), laid, laid, 23. lie (falsehood), lied, lied; 24. lie (intransitive), lay, lain; 25. loose, loosed, loosed; 26. lose, lost, lost; 27. mean, meant, meant; 28. pay, paid, paid; 29. plead, pleaded, pleaded; 30. prove, proved, proved; 31. put, put, put; 32. read, read, read; 33. ride, rode, ridden; 34. rise, rose, risen; 35. see, saw, seen; 36. set (transitive), set, set; 37. sit (intransitive), sat, sat; 38. sleep, slept, slept; 39. speak, spoke, spoken; 40. spring, sprang, sprung; 41. stride, strode, stridden; 42. swing, swung, swung; 43. tear, tore, torn; 44. thrive, throve, thrived; 45. tread, trod, trodden; 46. wear, wore, worn; 47. win, won, won; 48. wind, wound, wound; 49. wring, wrung, wrung; 50. write, wrote, written.

Hint 23. Check that you are using the correct principal part of the verb.
    Wrong: I *drawed* a pretty picture (drew).
            He *fit* a good fight (fought).
            I have *went* home (gone).
    Right: I *go* today; I *went* yesterday; I *have gone* often.

WORK THE EXERCISE ON PAGE 35
(If necessary, use your dictionary)

Exercise 14

	Right answers for page 33	Your answers for page 35
Trial I Place R if right; W, if wrong:		
1. They hanged the prisoner on the tree.	A	( )
2. I hung my hat on the rack.	H	( )
3. He wringed his hands.	L	( )
4. If I'd a-knowed I could a-rode, I would a-went!	L	( )
5. He swam ashore.		( )
6. He laid the object down.		( )
7. He done his best.		( )
8. He has borne the heat of the day.	R	( )
9. He loosed his pocketbook.	W	( )
10. He shaked her hand.	R	( )
11. He hanged his hat on the nail.	W	( )
12. He arose and spoke.	R	( )
13. He lay on the couch five hours yesterday.	W	( )
14. Please set down in that chair.	R	( )
15. He began a difficult task.	R	( )

CHECK your answers with the right ones on page 37. Go ahead if you have missed none. If you have missed one or more, try

W
W R
R

Number wrong

Trial II   Place R if right; W, if wrong:

1. He done his full duty.		( )
2. I have lain on the couch all day.		( )
3. He said, "Lay there till I come back!"		( )
4. He set a red hen.		( )
5. Here I set till she came home.		( )
6. The sheriff hung the horse thief.		( )
7. He will lose his reward.	L	( )
8. I loosed the prisoner from his chains.	A	( )
9. He was borne in 1864.	H	( )
10. The cold weather burst a pipe.	L	( )
11. He wrang the towel dry.		( )
12. He winded his watch.		( )
13. He sprang to my aid.		( )
14. I seen him run down the street.	W	( )
15. He teared the letter open.	W	( )

AFTER MASTERY, TURN TO PAGE 36

R
R
W
R
W
R
W
W
W
R
W

Number wrong

[35]

Hints: Tense of Verbs Grammar

24.0 Verbs may change form to show number, person, voice, mood, and tense. We conjugate a verb when we present in definite form all these changes. Thus, a conjugation is the regular arrangement of all the forms of a verb. In Tables I and II of the Appendix, you will find the complete conjugation of the verb *be* and the verb *choose*. At the present time our emphasis is on *tense*.

24.1 Tense denotes time. The six tenses are the present, the past, the future, the present perfect, the past perfect, and the future perfect tense.

Hint 24. Use the correct tense to express precise time.
24.2 Present tense (present time): I *hear* him. He *sees* me.
    24.21 The present tense is also used to state something that is always true: Reading *makes* the scholar. Love *is* blind.
    24.22 The present tense is sometimes used to narrate past events as though they were present. This use is called the *historical present*. It should not be overworked.
        Example: Bang! Bang! Another Indian *bites* the dust!
24.3 Past tense (past time): I *heard* him yesterday.
24.4 Future tense (future time): I *shall hear* him tomorrow.
24.5 Present perfect tense (completed prior to the present, or started in the past and continuing in the present. Its sign is *have* or *has*): I *have answered* his letter. He *has been working* since seven o'clock.
24.6 Past perfect tense (completed prior to some past event; its sign is *had*): I *had answered* her letter before he wrote me.
24.7 Future perfect tense (a future act to be completed before some future time): I *shall have received* my mail by the time you will arrive.
Tense may be expressed in three forms: the simple, the progressive, or the emphatic.
24.80 Tense expressed in the simple form: I *see*. I *ran* a race.
24.81 Tense expressed in the progressive form: I *am seeing*. I *am running* a race. I *am answering* him.
24.82 Tense expressed in the emphatic form: I *do see*. I *do run*. I *do answer*.

Hint 25. Do not shift tense needlessly.
    Wrong: He struck but *misses* the ball (missed).
           I go and he *followed* me (follows).
           I speak to him and he *acted* queerly (acts).

NOW WORK EXERCISE 15

Exercise 15

Trial I Indicate by proper number the tense of the italicized verbs (1. present; 2. past; 3. future; 4. present perfect; 5. past perfect; 6. future perfect):

Right answers for page 35 | Your answers for page 37

1. I came, I *saw*, I conquered. R ( )
2. The sun *shines* bright in my old Kentucky home. R ( )
3. I *shall come* next Thursday. W ( )
4. It *will be* a long time before he sings again. W ( )
5. He *had written* me last month. R ( )
6. By that time he *will have telephoned* me. R ( )
7. I *have forgotten* his rudeness. W ( )
8. She stirs! She starts! She *moves*! R ( )

Place R if right; W, if wrong:

W
W
W

9. I would fish every morning and every afternoon swam. R ( )
10. What is so rare as a day in June? R ( )
11. He came to bat and strikes out! W ( )
12. He has been calling me every hour. R ( )
13. I do like to hear him sing. ( )
14. It was a clear case she done him wrong. ( )
15. Rest for an hour and then you should go to work. ( )

CHECK your answers with the right ones on page 39. Go ahead if you have missed none. If you have missed one or more, try

W

Trial II IDENTIFY italicized words as in Trial I: R
W

1. He *will have forgotten* me by morning. R ( )
2. I *shall do* my duty. W ( )
3. He *sees* everything. W ( )
4. He *did* his best. R ( )
5. I *have answered* every question. R ( )
6. I *am* in earnest. W ( )
7. I *had replied* to his question. R ( )
8. Before the troops arrive, they *will have shot* him. W ( )

Place R if right; W, if wrong.

W
R
W

9. Honesty is the best policy. W ( )
10. I nod. He nods. He went home. ( )
11. I eats my breakfast regular. ( )
12. I weep and then he turns me down. ( )
13. The rain fell steadily since yesterday. ( )
14. I am happy to have seen you. ( )
15. Sculpture is a fine art. ( )

AFTER MASTERY, TURN TO PAGE 38

[37]

Hints: Particular Problem Verbs — Grammar

26.0   In English we have some troublesome verbs that have long bothered students of English. They are *lie, lay; sit, set; shall* and *will.*

26.1   *Lie* is an intransitive verb meaning to rest. Its principal parts are *lie, lay, lain.* Its correct use is as follows:
- Present tense: I *lie* on the couch today.
- Past tense: I *lay* there yesterday.
- Past participle: I *have lain* there often during my vacation.
- Present participle: The book is *lying* on the desk.
- Present gerund: *Lying* on the couch is pleasant.

26.2   *Lay* is a transitive verb, requires an object, and means to put or place. Its principal parts are *lay, laid, laid.* Its correct use is as follows:
- Present tense: I *lay* the book down today.
- Past tense: I *laid* it down yesterday.
- Past participle: I have *laid* it down often.
- Present participle and present gerund: *laying.*

26.3   *Sit* is an intransitive verb, meaning to rest in an upright position. Its three principal parts are *sit, sat, sat.* Its correct use is as follows:
- Present tense: I *sit* on the sofa today.
- Past tense: I *sat* there yesterday.
- Past participle: I have *sat* there often.
- Present participle and present gerund: *sitting.*

26.4   *Set* is a transitive verb, takes an object, and means to put or place. Its three principal parts are set, set, set. Its correct use is as follows:
- Present tense: I *set* the box down.
- Past tense: I *set* it down yesterday.
- Past participle: I have *set* it down often.
- Present participle and present gerund: *setting.*

26.5   *Shall* and *will, should* and *would* in the older grammars had numerous confusing rules which were not observed by many good writers. We are reducing these to the following basic principles for those who wish to retain the original distinction:

26.6   To express future action:

I shall go	We shall go
You will go	You will go
He will go	They will go

26.7   To express determination:

I will go	We will go
You shall go	You shall go
He shall go	They shall go

26.8   *Should* follows the same rules as *shall,* and *would* follows the same rule as *will:* I *should* answer. He *would* go.

Hint 26. Use *lie, lay, sit, set, shall,* and *will* correctly in all their forms.

NOW WORK EXERCISE 16

Exercise 16

	Right answers for page 37	Your answers for page 39

Trial I Place R if right; W, if wrong:

1. I shall call on you tomorrow. — 2 — ( )
2. Let it lay. — 1 — ( )
3. Now I lay me down to sleep. — 3 — ( )
4. She was sitting on the porch. — 3 — ( )
5. She lays around all day. — 5 — ( )
6. I shall set my burden down. — 6 — ( )
7. Will you do this for me? — 4 — ( )
8. I set the hen on a dozen eggs. — 1 — ( )
9. I set there at 8:00 p.m. — ( )
10. The sun sets early. (Better see your dictionary on this one!) — ( )
11. I will do my best. — ( )
12. I have often laid there. — W — ( )
13. I do plan the work that lies ahead. — R — ( )
14. She will order all the materials. — W — ( )
15. Please set down. — R — ( )

Right answers for page 37 (continued): R W R W W W

CHECK your answers with the right ones on page 41. Go ahead if you have missed none. If you have missed one or more, try

Number wrong _____

Trial II Place R if right; W, if wrong:

1. I am determined. He shall do it. — ( )
2. I should know better. — ( )
3. There he set, like a lump on a log. — ( )
4. I have been laying around all day. — 6 — ( )
5. Yes, he should have the chance. — 3 — ( )
6. Shall you go with me? — 1 — ( )
7. He was setting there resting. — 2 — ( )
8. They both will attend the opera. — 4 — ( )
9. All he did was set and eat. — 1 — ( )
10. May I sit here? — 5 — ( )
11. Let him lie where he fell. — 6 — ( )
12. If you would go, he would go. — ( )
13. He spent his life laying and setting around. — ( )
14. Set me down gently. — ( )
15. I shall see him face to face. — R — ( )

AFTER MASTERY, TURN TO PAGE 40

Right answers (continued): W W R W W R

Number wrong _____

Hints: Agreement of Subject and Predicate

27.0 Agreement is a correspondence between parts of a sentence. A verb should agree with its subject in number and person. Thus both verb and subject should be plural or both should be singular.

Hint 27. Be sure the verb agrees with the subject and not with some other word.

27.1 An intervening word sometimes misleads.
　　Wrong: The height of the mountains *astonish* the beholder.
　　Right: The height of the mountains *astonishes* the beholder. (*Height* is the subject—not *mountains*, and *height* is singular)

27.2 Singular pronouns, such as *everybody, another, anyone, each, nobody*, require singular verbs:
　　Wrong: Everybody should do *their* duty (his).

27.3 Two or more subjects joined by *and* take a plural verb; two or more singular subjects joined by *or* take a singular verb: John and I *are* going. Either John or Jim *is* going.

27.4 A collective noun takes a singular verb when the subject is thought of as a whole, but it takes a plural verb if the parts of the collective noun are being considered: The team *is* in good shape. The team *are* quarreling among themselves.

27.5 The expletive *there* is an introductory word which throws the subject later in the sentence. The verb agrees with this subject and not with *there*. The verb is plural or singular depending on this subject: There *were* many people present. There *is* a large crowd outside.

27.6 When two subjects differ in number or person and are joined by *or* or *nor*, the verb agrees with the nearer one: Neither the girls nor the dean *cares* to go.

27.7 Relative pronouns, such as *who, which, that*, are plural if their antecedents are plural and singular if their antecedents are singular: The club elected its officers, who *conduct* the operation.

27.8 The verb should agree with its subject and not necessarily with its subjective complement.
　　Wrong: Students *is* the teacher's main interest.
　　Right: Students *are* the teacher's main interest.

27.9 Some subjects are plural in form but singular in meaning. Of course they take a singular verb. If you are in doubt whether a word is plural or singular, check in your dictionary.
　　Examples: The news *is* good. Mathematics *is* an easy subject. Scissors *are* expensive. Trousers *cost* money.

NOW WORK EXERCISE ON PAGE 41

Exercise 17

Trial I Place R if right; W, if wrong:

		Right answers for page 39	Your answers for page 41
1.	The wages of Sin is death.	R	( )
2.	Five dollars is the price.	W	( )
3.	These pliers are expensive.	R	( )
4.	There are seven sons in this family.	R	( )
5.	Six brothers and one sister are attending.	W	( )
6.	The story of the travelers are interesting.	R	( )
7.	It are the leaders who know best.	R	( )
8.	Neither the brothers nor the sister are busy.	R	( )
9.	The club are unanimous.	W	( )
10.	Each should do their duty.	R	( )
11.	The sound of the singers disturbs the class.	R	( )
12.	The brother or the sister are going.	W	( )
13.	There were two hundred men present.	R	( )
14.	These are the men who carries the orders.	R	( )
15.	Girls, ugly or pretty, attracts his eye.	W	( )

Number wrong _____

CHECK your answers with the right ones on page 43. If you miss none, go ahead. If you miss one or more, try

Trial II Place R if right; W, if wrong:

1.	Athletics are important in the student's life.	R	( )
2.	Sports is the center of his thoughts.	R	( )
3.	The citizens elected men who are honest.	W	( )
4.	The depth of the waters interfere with the passage.	W	( )
5.	Nobody did their share.	R	( )
6.	Neither the sisters nor their brother sings.	R	( )
7.	There is many children in this crowd.	W	( )
8.	The committee disagree among themselves.	R	( )
9.	The team votes unanimously for Jim as captain.	W	( )
10.	Mary and Jane go to East High School.	R	( )
11.	He told the officers who runs the business.	R	( )
12.	The staff orders the meals.	R	( )
13.	The staff are divided on this issue.	W	( )
14.	The exterior of the boxes are beautiful.	R	( )
15.	Life is real; life is earnest.	R	( )

AFTER MASTERY, TURN TO PAGE 42

Number wrong _____

Hints: Verb, Mood   Grammar

28.0   The mood (or mode) of a verb indicates the state of mind in which a statement is made. English has three moods—the indicative, the imperative, and the subjunctive. In the informal use of English, the subjunctive mood is often replaced by the indicative. Other states of mind, such as compulsion, permission, obligation, are expressed by the proper auxiliary verb in connection with the verb.

28.1   The Indicative Mood expresses a fact or a question: He *came* early. *Are* you *willing? Must* we *answer?* He *can call* us.

28.2   The Imperative Mood expresses a command, a request, or an order: *Go* ahead (The subject *you* is understood). *Call* me. You *must advance* at once!

28.3   The Subjunctive Mood (when used) expresses a contrary to fact condition, a doubt, a supposition, necessity, parliamentary motions, a wish, or a recommendation.

         Contrary to fact: If I *were* chairman, I would report.
         A doubt or supposition: Suppose he *were* elected.
         Necessity: The teacher demanded that he *do* his homework.
         Parliamentary motion: Resolved, that he *be* secretary.
         Wish: I wish he *were* coming.
         Recommendation: Thy will *be* done.

28.4   The subjunctive mood of most verbs differs from the indicative in only the third person singular of the present tense and is formed by dropping the *s:* He comes. If he *come,* I will not go.

28.5   The verb *be* is a special problem. The subjunctive of *be* uses *be* in all forms of the present tense, *were* in the past tense, and *have been* in the present perfect tense. See Table II in the Appendix for the conjugation of *be* in the subjunctive mood.

Hint 28. Do not shift mood carelessly or needlessly.

This is consistent with the principle of Parallelism—like thought, like structure.

         Wrong: Hit and then you should run.
         Right: Hit and run.
         Wrong: If I were in your job and was dropped, I should feel sad.
         Right: If I were in your job and were dropped, I should feel sad.

NOW WORK EXERCISE 18
(Assume the use of the subjunctive)

Exercise 18

		Right answers for page 41	Your answers for page 43
Trial I	IDENTIFY by placing the proper number in parentheses (1. indicative; 2. imperative; 3. subjunctive):		

1. If this be treason, make the most of it.   R
2. Blow! Blow, thou Winter Wind!   R
3. The world is too much with us.   R
4. Will you call for me early?   R

Place R if right; W, if wrong:

5. I wish I was a little bird.   W   ( )
6. I count him among my important friends.   W   ( )
7. If I was you, I would be kind to her.   W   ( )
8. It was voted that John be chairman.   R   ( )
9. I recommend that John's expenses be paid.   W   ( )
10. Hit the first ball he throws.   R   ( )
11. Go and then you should wait for me.   W   ( )
12. I came, I saw, I conquered.   W   ( )
13. Spare if you will this old gray head.   ( )
14. May every wish be granted!   ( )
15. If he was in charge, I would go.   ( )

CHECK your answers with the right ones on page 45. If you miss none, go ahead. If you miss one or more, try

Number wrong

Trial II   IDENTIFY as in Trial I: R
                                         R

1. They also serve who only stand and wait.   R   ( )
2. Cast thy bread upon the waters.   W   ( )
3. Superstition is the religion of feeble minds.   W   ( )
4. If this be true, then all the world is false.   R   ( )

Place R if right; W, if wrong: R
                                 R

5. It was ordered that he be our leader.   W   ( )
6. I wish I was in Dixie.   R   ( )
7. A man's home is his castle.   R   ( )
8. Hail to the chief who in triumph advances.   W   ( )
9. I wish she were going.   R   ( )
10. Suppose he was chosen.   ( )
11. Call me if you want me.   ( )
12. Stop and then you should look and listen.   ( )
13. If I were greeted and then I was laughed at, I would be angry too.   ( )
14. Resolved, that the meeting adjourn.   ( )
15. If I were he, I wouldn't answer.   ( )

AFTER MASTERY, TURN TO PAGE 44

Number wrong

Hints: Verbs, Voice Grammar

29.0 Voice shows whether the subject of the sentence or clause is acting or being acted upon. In the active voice of the verb, the subject is the doer; in the passive voice the subject has something done to it. Only transitive verbs may be expressed in the passive voice.
    Active voice: She *gave* me a book. (past tense)
    Passive voice: A book *was given* me by her. (past tense)
    Active voice: Our class *works* problems. (present tense)
    Passive voice: Problems *are worked* by our class. (present tense)

29.1 The choice of voice depends whether the doer or the receiver should come first and be emphasized. Note what happens to the subjects and the complements when we change from the active to the passive voice:

    Active voice: My   *boss*   gave   me   my   *pay*
                  (subject)   (indirect   (direct
                               object)   object)

    Passive voice: *I*   *was given*   my *pay*   by the   *boss.*
                 (subject)   (retained   (object of
                                     object)   preposition)

    Passive voice: My *pay*   *was given*   me   by my   *boss*
                 (subject)   (indirect   (object of
                                   object)   preposition)

29.2 The passive voice may be used (1) to emphasize the receiver of the action; (2) to state a generalization; or (3) to maintain an impersonal viewpoint.
    Emphasis: This promotion *was received* joyfully.
    Generalization: This truth *has been proved* many times.
    Impersonal viewpoint: The following facts *were obtained* in this study.

29.3 The passive voice may be used in the simple and progressive forms of the conjugation, but it does not appear in the emphatic form.
    Simple form: It *was seen* in the distance.
    Progressive form: It *was being seen* in various parts of the city.

29.4 See the conjugation of *be* and *choose* in Tables I and II of the Appendix.

Hint 29. Prefer the active voice.
    Passive voice: The game *was won* by our team.
    Active voice: Our team *won* the game.

Exercise 19

Trial I IDENTIFY italicized verbs by placing in the parentheses A for active voice and P for passive voice:

		Right answers for page 43	Your answers for page 45
1.	It *has been driven* over fifty thousand miles.	3	( )
2.	He *threw* me the ball.	2	( )
3.	No one *is permitted* to enter.	1	( )
4.	She *is cleaning* the kitchen.	1	( )
5.	*Bring* me my uniform.		( )
6.	The flowers *were arranged* by my sister.		( )
7.	The play *will have been given* by that time.		( )
8.	The team *was being defeated* by our opponents.	W	( )
9.	I *do believe* him.	R	( )
10.	*Play* ball.	W	( )

Place S if strong; W, if weak:

		R	
		R	
11.	The game was lost by me.	W	( )
12.	His courage has been proved a thousand times.	R	( )
13.	We will fight and we will win.	R	( )
14.	This was seen clearly by him.	R	( )
15.	I hope he will return.	W	( )

CHECK your answers with the right ones on page 47. If you miss none, go ahead. If you miss one or more, try

Number wrong

Trial II IDENTIFY in the same manner as in Trial I:

1.	The reply *has been received*.	1	( )
2.	He *will be accepted* with pride.	2	( )
3.	He *is cheering* merrily.	1	( )
4.	I *do insist* that he go.	3	( )
5.	It *might have been*.		( )
6.	The deed *had been done* in broad daylight.		( )
7.	This truth *has been known* for many years.		( )
8.	*Tell* him not to do it.	R	( )
9.	He *is cheering* loudly.	W	( )
10.	*Don't be cheated!*	R	( )

Place S if strong; W, if weak:

		R	
		R	
		W	
11.	It was decided by him that I should go.	R	( )
12.	The ship should not be given up by us.	W	( )
13.	I call for immediate action.	W	( )
14.	Let us fight like men.	R	( )
15.	The smile was given me by a pretty lass.	R	( )

AFTER MASTERY, TURN TO PAGE 46

Number wrong

Review

Grammar

It's time for another backward look.

If you care to, review all errors or difficulties since the last test.

Grade yourself on your first attempt, using the previous scale. You will recall this is the scale:

ERRORS	GRADE
0 - 2	A
3 - 4	B
5 - 6	C
7 - 8	D
More than 8	F, or failed

You are making good progress if you make less than three errors on this test. If you make three or more, review till you are sure of mastery. By this time you know how "to put oil where the squeaks are." Note the right answers in the Key on page 49 and references to the Hint for each item missed.

NOW DO THE TEST ON PAGE 47
(I hope sincerely that you will do well!)

Review Test III

Review Test III IDENTIFY by appropriate number the italicized words (1. linking verb; 2. transitive verb; 3. auxiliary verb):

		Right answers for page 45	Your answers for page 47
1.	He *has knocked* a home run.	P	( )
2.	It *sounds* good.	A	( )
3.	I *do* believe you.	P	( )

For the following italicized words, use these symbols: 1. present tense; 2. past tense; 3. future tense; 4. present perfect tense; 5. past perfect tense; 6. future perfect tense.

		A A P P P	
4.	He *will come* at dawn.	A	( )
5.	I *had mailed* the letter.	A	( )
6.	I *am going* home.		( )
7.	He *disappeared* yesterday.		( )
8.	Before we get there, he *will have gone*.		( )

For the following, use these symbols: 1. indicative mood; 2. imperative mood; 3. subjunctive mood.

		W S S W	
9.	I wish she *were* my secretary.	S	( )
10.	*Are* you *attending* the game?		( )
11.	*Drop* your gun and surrender!		( )
12.	Night's candles *are burnt* out.		( )

Place R if right; W, if wrong:

13.	I would of gone if I had been you.	P	( )
14.	It sounds loudly because he plays loud.	P	( )
15.	The peach smells ripe.	A	( )
16.	They hung the victim on the tree.	A	( )
17.	He loosed his watch.	P	( )
18.	Every day he lays on that truck.	P	( )
19.	I sit and sit, and nothing happens.	P	( )
20.	I talk to him, and he insulted me.	A	( )
21.	I have laid on the couch a long time.	A	( )
22.	Tomorrow I shall go.	P	( )
23.	I set the clock on the shelf.		( )
24.	I lie in bed and think.		( )
25.	The speed of the rivers astonish me.		( )
26.	There was many fans present.	W	( )
27.	This news is recent.	W	( )
28.	Stop and then you should look and listen.	S	( )
29.	If I was you, I would try to do better.	S	( )
30.	Dare to be a man!	W	( )

AFTER MASTERY, TURN TO PAGE 48

Number wrong _____

Grade _____

Hints: Verbals   Grammar

30.0   A verbal is derived from a verb but it can not do the job of a verb. Thus it is the source of many errors. It has the nature of a verb in many respects, but often its other nature as some other part of speech is more important than its verb nature. It is important to remember that a verbal is a word with the dual nature of a verb and some other part of speech. It can act as a noun, adjective, or adverb, and its verbal nature can take modifiers. It can not make a statement. It can not be a predicate. It can take an object, have tense and voice, and be modified by adverbs.

30.1   There are three kinds of verbals—participles, gerunds, and infinitives:
     30.11   A participle is a verbal adjective:
         Frowning fiercely, he glared at us.
         Having been defeated, the army retreated to Rome.
     30.12   A gerund is a verbal noun:
         Going home is pleasant.
         They told of his *having been arrested.*
     30.13   An infinitive is a verbal which may be used as a noun, adjective, or adverb. It is usually preceded by *to,* its sign:
         Used as a noun: *To fish* is great sport.
         Used as an adjective: His ambition *to work* had everyone's approval.

Hint 30. Do not mistake a verbal for a verb

A review of our discussion of Fragments, page 8, would show that unjustifiable fragments often use verbals, but sentences must have verbs.

Verbs and verbals differ also in their relationship to time. The verb has its own time; the verbal's time is always dependent on that of the verb. It is good to remember that the verbal depends in many ways on some verb.

     Wrong: *Frowning* fiercely in the morning's sunshine.
     Right: He was frowning in the morning's sunshine.
     Wrong: *Singing* carols in the snow at Christmas.
     Right: Singing carols in the snow at Christmas is timely.
     Wrong: *To do* your duty in every situation.
     Right: To do your duty in every situation is expected.

WORK THE EXERCISE ON PAGE 49

Exercise 20

Trial I   IDENTIFY by appropriate letter the italicized verbals (G for gerund; I for infinitive; P for participle):

	Right answers for page 47	Your answers for page 49
1. She objected to his *going* to college.	2–6.11	( )
2. *Fuming* in anger, he approached the teacher.	1–21.1	( )
3. *To be* or not to be—that is the question.	3–22.1	( )
4. John, *having lost* his place, went to the rear.		( )
5. His *leaving* his place caused all this trouble.		( )
6. There was a discussion concerning his *returning*.		( )
7. He surely intended *to go*.		( )
8. It was indeed a treat *to have heard* her.		( )
9. Slowly *sinking*, the sun sent forth its rays.	3–24.4	( )

Place R if right; W, if wrong:

5–24.6
1–24.2
2–24.3

10. Going home in the dark of the evening.	6–24.7	( )
11. We are starting early in the day.		( )
12. To have replied angrily in the first place.		( )
13. Arising before the sun appeared in its bright glory.		( )
14. To act so is treason.		( )
15. I love to tell the story.	3–28.3	( )

1–28.1
2–28.2
1–28.1

CHECK your answers with the right ones on page 51. If you miss none, go ahead. If you miss one or more, try

Number wrong

Trial II   IDENTIFY as in Trial I:

1. This delayed his *answering* my letter.	W–22.0	( )
2. It is better *to have loved* and lost than never to have loved at all.	W–21.3	( )
3. *Working* steadily, he sticks to his difficult job.	R–21.3	( )
4. Jim, *having answered* my letter, returned to his cabin.	W–23.4	( )
5. He always tries *to do* his best.	W–23.4	( )
6. *To run* away is cowardly.	W–26.1	( )
7. *Attending* classes at 7:00 a.m. is not easy.	R–26.3	( )
8. *Smiling* broadly, he walked up to the lady.	W–25.0	( )
9. That act was his *undoing*.	W–26.1	( )

R–26.5

Place R if right; W, if wrong:

R–26.4
R–26.1

10. Always striving to be the best in his class.	W–27.1	( )
11. Set a thief to catch a thief.	W–27.5	( )
12. His stopping us on the main highway.	R–27.9	( )
13. Time brings the truth to light.	W–28.0	( )
14. Stepping forward as a hero should.	W–28.3	( )
15. To answer every question on the test.	R–28.2	( )

AFTER MASTERY, TURN TO PAGE 50

Number wrong

Hints: Participles and Gerunds   Grammar

31.0   Participles and gerunds are verbals, dependent upon some verb in the sentence. If the verbal acts also as an adjective, it is a participle; if it acts also as a noun, it is a gerund. Participles and gerunds often are identical in form; usage determines their class. For their conjugation, see Table II of the Appendix.

31.1   As stated above, the use of the verbal determines its class:
Active Voice:
> Participle, present tense: *Choosing* to go, John called me.
> Gerund, present tense: His *choosing* to go pleased me.
> Participle, perfect tense: John, *having chosen* me, dismissed the others.
> Gerund, perfect tense: His *having chosen* me discouraged the others.
> (Note that neither the participle nor the gerund has a past tense in the active voice.)

Passive Voice:
> Participle, present tense: John, *being chosen,* accepted the position.
> Gerund, present tense: His *being chosen* was expected.
> Participle, past tense: John, *chosen* by ballot, became the chairman.
> Gerund, past tense: (This form does not appear.)
> Participle, perfect tense: John, *having been chosen,* stated his program.
> Gerund, perfect tense: His *having been chosen* surprised everyone.

31.2   The gerund as a noun can be modified by an adjective, and can be the subject or the object of a verb or the object of a preposition; as a verb it can take an object and be modified by an adverb:
> He enjoyed *giving* gifts to the poor. (The gerund *giving* is the object of enjoyed, takes the object *gifts,* and is modified by the adverbial phrase *to the poor.*)
> Gladly *giving* gifts was a long habit. (Giving is a subject, it takes the object *gifts,* and is modified by *gladly.*)

31.3   A problem may arise whether a verbal is a gerund or a participle. If the emphasis is on the action, the verbal is a gerund, and good usage prefers the possessive case of the noun or pronoun; if the emphasis is on the noun or pronoun, the verbal is a participle, and the noun or pronoun may be in the nominative or objective case:
> Gerund: His *entering* the room caused the confusion.
> Participle: He heard me *calling* him.
> Gerund: He came without my *calling* him.
> Participle: We caught him *entering* the room.

Hint 31. Prefer the possessive case for the noun or pronoun closely linked with a gerund

NOW TURN TO THE EXERCISE ON PAGE 51

Exercise 21

Trial I   IDENTIFY by appropriate number the use of the italicized gerund in each of these sentences (1. subject; 2. subjective complement; 3. direct object; 4. object of a preposition):

	Right answers for page 49	Your answers for page 51
1. I tried to get there by *speeding*.	G	( )
2. *Running* the mile requires training.	P	( )
3. He enjoyed *buying* gifts for his friends.	I	( )
4. His weakness is always *asking* questions.	P	( )
5. He objected to my *bartering* trifles.	G	( )

Mark A if in the active voice; mark P if in the passive voice:

	G	
	I	
6. *Having bought* the car, he drove it away.	P	( )
7. *Acknowledged* as leader, he assumed command.	P	( )
8. His *having been recognized* spoiled our plans.		( )
9. The critics declared his *acting* to be superb.		( )
10. *Being dismissed*, the students left the hall.		( )

Mark R if right; W, if wrong:

	W	
	R	
	W	
11. I heard him whistling in the dark.	W	( )
12. His answering me so promptly showed his sincerity.	R	( )
13. I miss him singing in our glee club.	R	( )
14. He does not like me doing better.		( )
15. He praised our *helping* others.		( )

CHECK your answers with the right ones on page 53. If you miss none, go ahead. If you miss one or more, try

Number wrong

Trial II   IDENTIFY sentence use as in Trial I:

1. He praised me for my *singing*.	G	( )
2. He likes *reading* poetry.	I	( )
3. The main job in college is *studying*.	P	( )
4. His intention is *marrying* the girl.	P	( )
5. His *declining* to answer showed his guilt.	I	( )

Identify voice as in Trial I:

	I	
	G	
	P	
6. *Punished* for his deed, he ran away.	G	( )
7. *Skating* is pleasant in winter.		( )
8. His *hoping* ended in despair.		( )
9. *Having been praised*, he was happy.		( )
10. *Delighted* with the results, he went to the store.		( )

Place R if right; W, if wrong:

	W	
	R	
	W	
11. He saw Alfred smiling at her.	R	( )
12. He resented Joe's asking her to the party.	W	( )
13. It was him drinking that worried his mother.	W	( )
14. We admired his advancing so rapidly.		( )
15. We laughed at him dodging the issue.		( )

AFTER MASTERY, TURN TO PAGE 52

Number wrong

Hints: Infinitives — Grammar

32.0 An infinitive is a verbal which may be used as a noun, an adjective, or an adverb. It is often introduced by the sign *to*, but sometimes this sign is omitted. It appears in both the present and the perfect tenses, active and passive voice.

> As noun and subject: *To swim* is fun.
> As noun and object: Charles wants *to go*.
> As noun and subjective complement: His promise was *to call* me.
> As noun and object of a preposition: He is about *to answer*.
> As an adjective: His right *to command* was not questioned.
> As an adjective: He had the willingness *to help*.
> As an adverb: This game is difficult *to play*.
> As an adverb: I am pleased *to see* you.

32.1 The subject of an infinitive is in the objective case. The object and the objective complement of an infinitive are also in this case. Watch particularly the case of pronouns as they often cause trouble:

> They asked *him to run* for office.
> They made *him do* it. (Here *do* is an infinitive without its sign, *to*)
> Whom did he take *her to be?* (*Whom* must agree with *her*)
> Did he think *her to be* me? (Note the correct form *me* as objective complement after *her*.)

Hint 32. Avoid the split infinitive unless clarity demands it.
When words, phrases, or even clauses come between *to* and the verb of the infinitive, this construction is known as a *split infinitive*. Many reputable writers use the split infinitive, generally with only an adverb closely connected to the verb. However, it is good practice to avoid a long and awkward insertion between *to* and the verb:

> Wrong: He asked us *to as soon as possible call* him.
> Weak: *To merely see* her was happiness.
> Weak: She tries *to distinctly speak*.
> Right: He asked us to call him as soon as possible.
> Right: Merely to see her was happiness.
> Right: She tries to speak distinctly.
> Acceptable: The lady seemed to have *just* arrived.

NOW TURN TO EXERCISE 22

Exercise 22

Trial I   IDENTIFY with appropriate number the use in the sentence of the italicized infinitives (1. subject; 2. object; 3. subjective complement; 4. object of a preposition; 5. adjective; 6. adverb):

		Right answers for page 51	Your answers for page 53
1.	He was happy *to promote* him.	4	( )
2.	His aim is *to succeed*.	1	( )
3.	He wanted *to reach* the top.	3	( )
4.	He had a tendency *to irritate* friends.	2	( )
5.	*To try* your best is all that we can ask.	4	( )
6.	His ability *to argue* was well known.		( )
7.	Wounds made by words are hard *to heal*.		( )
8.	He seemed about *to ask* us.	A	( )

Place R if right; W, if wrong:

		P P A P	
9.	The student should remember to not frequently and carelessly split an infinitive.		( )
10.	Who do you take her to be?		( )
11.	They asked her to do it.		( )
12.	He needs to learn the lesson thoroughly.	R	( )
13.	Did he take him to be I?	R	( )
14.	He wished to substantially and exactly prove his point.	W	( )
15.	He hoped to demonstrate it precisely.	W R	( )

CHECK your answers with the right ones on page 55. If you miss none, go ahead. If you miss one or more, try

Number wrong

Trial II   Identify as in Trial I:

		4	
1.	We should learn *to rule* ourselves.	3	( )
2.	He seemed *to be* guilty.	2	( )
3.	No way remains except *to go* on.	2	( )
4.	I have a duty *to perform*.	1	( )
5.	*To err* is human.		( )
6.	Such wounds are hard *to heal*.		( )
7.	He has a place *to fill* in this world.	P	( )
8.	We try *to please*.	A	( )

Place R if right; W, if wrong:

		A P P	
9.	He planned to courteously and graciously meet her.	P	( )
10.	He seems to have just made a decision.		( )
11.	Did he think she to be I?		( )
12.	Then who did he think her to be?	R	( )
13.	To be silent is a poor answer to slander.	R	( )
14.	I attempted to sweetly, gently, and humbly answer her.	W	( )
15.	I come not here to talk.	R W	( )

AFTER MASTERY, TURN TO PAGE 54

Number wrong

[53]

Hints: Dangling Verbals — Grammar

33.0   A dangling modifier is one which wrongly modifies one word when actually it should modify another. This confusion leaves it dangling, misunderstood, and often ridiculous. Our verbals, the participle, the gerund, and the infinitive, often find themselves in this mess.

33.1   The participle.
       Wrong: *Turning* left, the gym is seen.
       Right: If you turn left, you can see the gym.
       Wrong: *Having rotted* on the tree, my brother could find no apples.
       Right: My brother could find no apples because they had rotted on the tree.
       Wrong: Busily engaged in *gnawing a nut,* we saw a squirrel near the top of the tree.
       Right: We saw a squirrel busily engaged in gnawing a nut.

33.2   The gerund.
       Wrong: In *buying* a car, the reputation of the dealer should be considered.
       Right: In buying a car, one should consider the reputation of the dealer.
       Wrong: After *moving* to Florida, my cough disappeared.
       Right: After moving to Florida, I lost my cough.

33.3   The infinitive.
       Wrong: *To appreciate* art, the picture must be studied.
       Right: To appreciate art, one must study the picture.
       Wrong: *To succeed,* the game must be played carefully.
       Right: To succeed, one must play the game carefully.

Hint 33. Avoid dangling verbals.
Always place verbals so that the meaning is clear. Sometimes this will require a careful rewording of the sentence or making the verbal a member of a compound predicate.
       Wrong: *Running* down the street, the police station came to view.
       Right: Running down the street, we saw the police station.
       Wrong: In *hurrying* away, the girl was avoided.
       Right: He avoided the girl by hurrying away.
       Wrong: *To belong* to the team, the coach must be satisfied.
       Right: To belong to the team, you must satisfy the coach.

NOW TURN TO EXERCISE 23

Exercise 23

		Right answers for page 53	Your answers for page 55
Trial I	Place R if right; W, if wrong:		
1.	The leader told us to as loud as possible shout.	6	( )
2.	Having bought a newspaper, the newsboy directed me to my hotel.	3	( )
3.	The blood stirs more to raise a lion than to start a hare.	2	( )
4.	England expects every man to do his duty.	5	( )
5.	To play tennis, the eye must be kept on the ball.	1	( )
6.	He was pleased to more definitely outline the problem.	5	( )
7.	Walking through the park, I saw many birds.	6	( )
8.	Many receive advice, but few profit from it.	4	( )
9.	Hanging from a branch, I saw a squirrel.		( )
10.	After shooting the bear, my nerve failed me.		( )
11.	Boxing is an excellent sport.		( )
12.	His flirting with girls is one of his weaknesses.		( )
13.	Him cheating in algebra caused his expulsion.	W	( )
14.	We laughed at his awkward dancing.	W	( )
15.	He promised to call me in the morning.	R	( )

CHECK your answers with the right ones on page 57. If you miss none, go ahead. If you miss one or more, try

R
W
W
W
R
R

Number wrong

Trial II	Place R if right; W, if wrong:		
1.	To be or not to be — that is the question.		( )
2.	He was pleased to have been heard.		( )
3.	In building a boat, blue prints are necessary.		( )
4.	He asked us to as soon as possible answer his letter.		( )
5.	His shouting so loudly aroused us.	2	( )
6.	Seeing is believing.	3	( )
7.	In ordering steak, the kind you want is important.	4	( )
8.	He had no plans except to do his best.	5	( )
9.	He tried to investigate the causes.	1	( )
10.	To start the fire, the paper should be ignited.	6	( )
11.	His acting brought him fame.	5	( )
12.	We praised him for his clever blocking.	2	( )
13.	To know this teacher was to honor her.		( )
14.	Enclosed with my order, you will find a check.		( )
15.	Sitting in my car, the elephant seemed immense.		( )

AFTER MASTERY, TURN TO PAGE 56

W
R
W
W
R
W
R

Number wrong

[55]

Hints: Other Misplaced Modifiers   Grammar

34.0   Other modifiers than verbals may dangle. Modifiers must be placed in the position where they fulfill their purpose clearly. In any other position they may become ludicrous.

34.1   Among the adverbs, *only, not, even,* and *hardly* need careful attention. This is true also of the correlative conjunctions *both – and, either –or, neither – nor, not only – but also.*
   Wrong: He *only* gave me a dollar.
   Right: He gave me *only* a dollar.
   Wrong: *Not only* is the job pleasant *but also* profitable.
   Right: The job is *not only* pleasant *but also* profitable.

34.2   Words, phrases, even clauses should be so arranged that the meaning of the sentence is clear:
   Wrong: He sold a green woman's hat.
   Right: He sold a woman's green hat.
   Wrong: Wanted – a room by a bachelor fully plastered.
   Right: Wanted – by a bachelor, a room fully plastered.
   Wrong: Many problems confront the importer of staples which must be solved.
   Right: Many problems which must be solved confront the importer of staples.

34.3   A dangling elliptical clause is one from which the subject or verb, or both, have been omitted (Ellipsis means omission). Confusion may result when these omitted words differ from those of the main clause:
   Wrong: When eight years old, my mother died.
   Right: When I was eight years old, my mother died.
   Wrong: While working this morning, the whistle blew.
   Right: While he was working this morning, the whistle blew.

34.4   Squinting modifiers are modifiers so placed in a sentence that they may be understood with either the preceding or the following words:
   Wrong: They agreed today to go home.
   Right: (Either) Today they agreed to go home; or, They agreed to go home today.
   Wrong: I climbed the mountain when the sun went down to see the beautiful colors in the sky.
   Right: (Either) When the sun went down, I climbed the mountain to see the beautiful colors;
       or, I climbed the mountain to see the beautiful colors when the sun went down.

Hint 34. Place all kinds of modifiers so intended meanings are clear.

NOW WORK EXERCISE 24

Exercise 24

		Right answers for page 55	Your answers for page 57
Trial I	Place R if right; W, if wrong:		
1.	He only wanted a quarter.	W	( )
2.	He not only bought a gun but he also purchased a bicycle.	W	( )
3.	After glancing at the menu, he ordered a hot bowl of soup.	R	( )
4.	The teacher demanded during the next day the work be completed.	R	( )
5.	When six years old, my grandmother gave me a watch.	W	( )
6.	He ought not to be permitted to drive a car.	W	( )
7.	With my own eyes I saw him strike out.	R	( )
8.	He is inclined to abide strictly by all rules.	R	( )
9.	The lad was neither kind nor docile.	W	( )
10.	He ordered a fried dish of bacon.	W	( )
11.	Who steals my purse steals trash.	R	( )
12.	They promised today to go hunting.	R	( )
13.	Youth is the time when the seeds of character are sown.	W	( )
14.	Our plane flew over the home where Washington lived last summer.	R	( )
15.	After we had stopped with the aid of the guide we found our way.	R	( )

CHECK your answers with the right ones on page 59. If you missed none, go ahead. If you missed one or more, try

Number wrong

Trial II	Place R if right; W, if wrong:		
1.	He must have certainly been ill.	R	( )
2.	We speak merely of numbers.	R	( )
3.	I caught a fish on a hook baited with a worm which we ate for lunch.	W	( )
4.	That tall man is speaking with long whiskers.	W	( )
5.	He agreed hastily to repair the damage.	R	( )
6.	When walking down the street, the car hit a tree.	R	( )
7.	One swallow does not make a summer.	W	( )
8.	Why waste a word or let a tear escape?	R	( )
9.	They asked him during the next month to give them a decision.	R	( )
10.	Having reached the age of thirteen, I decided to take my son along.	W	( )
11.	He almost ate the whole pie.	R	( )
12.	I tell sad stories of the death of kings.	R	( )
13.	Touch not, taste not, handle not.	R	( )
14.	I have neither the time nor the inclination to attend.	W	( )
15.	He knew a man with a wooden leg by the name of Smith.	W	( )

AFTER MASTERY, TURN TO PAGE 58

Number wrong

Hints: The Phrase — Grammar

35.0   A phrase is a group of related words lacking both subject and predicate. It is not a sentence, but a part of a sentence. It may be used as a noun, adjective, verb, or adverb. It should be remembered that a phrase is a "fragment" of a sentence and should not be used alone.

35.1   Phrases may be classified according to their use as noun, adjective, verb, or adverb phrases. Phrases may be classified according to their form as prepositional, participial, gerund, infinitive, or absolute phrases:

     35.11   A prepositional phrase consists of a preposition, its object, and modifiers. It may be used as an adjective, an adverb, or a noun:
        Used as an adjective: The tree *with its pretty red leaves* is a maple.
        Used as an adverb: He walked *with a limp.*
        Used as a noun: *After supper* is the time to see television.

     35.12   The participial phrase consists of a participle and related words. It acts as an adjective:
        Example: The man *holding the horse* is a cowboy.
        Example: The treasure *found in the sea* was distributed.

     35.13   The gerund phrase consists of a gerund and related words. It acts as a noun:
        As subject: *Chewing tobacco* is a bad habit.
        As object: The teacher condemned *chewing tobacco.*
        As subjective complement: His bad habit is *chewing tobacco.*
        As object of a preposition: He ruined his health by *chewing tobacco.*

     35.14   The infinitive phrase consists of an infinitive and related words. It may be used as a noun, adjective, or adverb:
        As noun: *To run away* is cowardly.
        As adjective: The wish *to run away* comes to us all.
        As adverb: He came *to greet us.*

     35.15   Two types of phrases do not dangle. The first of these is the *absolute phrase.* It consists of a noun followed and modified by a participle. It is called *absolute* because it does not modify the subject of the main clause. In Latin it is called the *ablative absolute;* in English, the *nominative absolute.* It does not dangle, but care must be exercised so it does not appear as a fragment.
        Examples: *The moon having risen,* we began to sing.
                 His job done, the carpenter picked up his tools.
        The second type of phrase that does not dangle is the idiomatic phrase that may express a generalization. It also does not modify the subject of the main clause.
        Examples: *Generally speaking,* English is difficult.
                 Failing assent, the chairman dismissed the group.
                 Taking everything into consideration, it still is not too late.

Hint 35. Place phrases so relationships are clear

NOW WORK EXERCISE 25

Exercise 25

Trial I IDENTIFY type of phrase of italicized words by placing appropriate number in the parentheses (1. prepositional; 2. participial; 3. gerund; 4. infinitive; 5. absolute):

Right answers for page 57 | Your answers for page 59

1. *The trial being over,* the judge dismissed the jury.
2. The queen *of the tournament* was a sophomore.
3. *His running for sheriff* worried his friends.
4. She tried *to swim* the English Channel.
5. The horse *purchased at the auction* won the race.
6. *In the morning* he worked in a grocery.

IDENTIFY the part of speech for which each phrase is used by placing the appropriate number in the parentheses (1. noun; 2. adjective; 3. adverb):

7. He studied *before going to bed.*
8. The girl *waving her hand* is my sister.
9. *Getting up in the morning* is not easy.
10. The trees, *dripping with icicles,* presented a pretty sight.

Place R if right; W, if wrong:

11. He expected in the early morning to shoot a deer.
12. Expecting an answer, the book was closed by the boy.
13. Sitting in my car, the bear approached me.
14. He was anxious to do his best.
15. The sun is very relaxing while swimming.

Right answers for page 57: W W W W W R R R R R W R W R W W R W W

CHECK your answers with the right ones on page 61. If you miss none, go ahead. If you miss one or more, try

Trial II IDENTIFY type of phrase as above:

1. His eagerness *to serve* was commendable.
2. *In the afternoon* he went golfing.
3. *This having been accomplished,* the army retreated.
4. The Christmas tree, *ornamented beautifully,* was attractive.
5. *His yelling for help* saved him.
6. *Her eyes gleaming,* she seemed happy.

IDENTIFY, as above, use as a part of speech:

7. He did calisthenics *before eating breakfast.*
8. The dog *barking at us* belongs to my neighbor.
9. He tried *sleeping on his back.*
10. His aim is *to please.*

Place R if right; W, if wrong:

11. Standing on the platform, the elephant was clearly seen.
12. He promised late at night to call on me.
13. Truth crushed to earth shall rise again.
14. While playing in the water, the boat was upset.
15. Generally speaking, women live longer than men.

Right answers for page 57 (Trial II): W R W W W W W W W R R W W R R R W

AFTER MASTERY, TURN TO PAGE 60

Your answers for page 59: ( ) for each of items 1–15 in Trial I, Number wrong ____; ( ) for each of items 1–15 in Trial II, Number wrong ____.

Hints: Clauses — Grammar

36.0   A clause is a group of words having a subject and a predicate. It may be a sentence or a part of a sentence. There are two kinds: independent (or *main* or *principal*) and dependent (or *subordinate*).

36.1   An independent clause makes sense when it stands alone. If it stands alone, it is a sentence.
         Example: Spring is pleasant.

36.2   A dependent clause can not make sense alone, and it is always part of a sentence. It is dependent on some other part of the sentence.
         Example: When summer comes, —.

36.3   There are three kinds of dependent clauses: the adjective clause; the adverb clause; and the noun clause.

36.4   The adjective clause acts as an adjective—it modifies a noun or pronoun:
         The soldiers *who fought in the war* returned home (modifies a noun).
         It came to him *who deserved it* (modifies a pronoun).

36.5   The adverb clause acts as an adverb. It may modify a verb, an adjective, or another adverb. It may indicate *place, manner, cause, purpose, condition, comparison, degree, result, concession, time*:
         Place: He lived *where land was cheap.*
         Manner: He acted *as if he knew better.*
         Cause: He subscribed *because he liked the paper.*
         Purpose: She came *in order that she might aid.*
         Comparison: He is stronger *than I (am strong).*
         Degree: She is just as pleased *as I am.*
         Result: He ate so much *that he became ill.*
         Concession: *Although you scorn me,* I will not leave you.
         Time: You may leave *when the bell rings.*

36.6   The noun clause acts as a noun, and may be used in all the ways a noun may be used. Often it can be recognized by an introductory *that*:
         Subject: *That he plays beautifully* is evident.
         Object: He demonstrated *that he knew the game.*
         Subjective complement: My promise is *that he will play.*
         Object of preposition: I am not aware of *what he might do.*

36.7   A common error is to use an adverbial clause as though it were a noun clause, using as introductory words *is when, is where,* and *is because:*
         Wrong: Scoring *is when* you make a goal.
         Right: Scoring is making a goal.

36.8   An elliptical dependent clause is one in which the subject and frequently part of the predicate are omitted because they are understood from the main clause:
         Elliptical: When in Columbus, he visited me.
         Full: When he was in Columbus, he visited me.

Hint 36. Identify clauses carefully.

NOW WORK EXERCISE 26

Exercise 26

Trial I   IDENTIFY these clauses as independent or dependent by placing the appropriate number in the parentheses (1. independent; 2. dependent):

	Right answers for page 59	Your answers for page 61
1. *That he will be our next president* is clear to all.	5	( )
2. This is the house *that Jack built*.	1	( )
3. *When the sun sets*, we shall return home.	3	( )
4. We looked for a restaurant *because we were hungry*.	4	( )

IDENTIFY use as part of speech (1. noun; 2. adjective; 3. adverb):

	2	
	1	
5. This is the house *that Jack built*.		( )
6. It was shown *that he really was a hero*.		( )
7. *When you send the bill*, I will pay it.		( )
8. He knew *that girls attract attention to themselves*.		( )

IDENTIFY type of adverb clause (1. manner; 2. concession; 3. purpose 4. degree; 5. time; 6. elliptical):

	3	
	2	
	1	
	2	
9. He knew the truth *although he failed to apply it*.		( )
10. *When hungry*, he rushed to the refrigerator.		( )

Place R if right; W, if wrong:

	W	
11. Whenever you get yourself into a mess of trouble.	W	( )
12. He knows in whom he has confidence.	W	( )
13. They agreed when the sun rose that he should start.	R	( )
14. This is the thing that I was born to do.	W	( )
15. He stood in deep snow looking at the barn which had fallen white and beautiful during the night.		( )

CHECK your answers with the right ones on page 63. If you miss none, go ahead. If you miss one or more, try

Number wrong ____

Trial II   IDENTIFY as independent or dependent as in Trial I:

	4	
	1	
1. We know *that he will come in time*;	5	( )
2. *Be true to your convictions*.	2	( )
3. *Because we liked him*, we invited him.	3	( )
4. *If you do your best*, you will pass this test.	5	( )

IDENTIFY usage as a part of speech as in Trial I:

5. *Although you tried*, you failed.		( )
6. The car *which he bought* was an old one.	3	( )
7. The fact is *that he leads his class*.	2	( )
8. He said *that you will remember him*.	1	( )
9. *Although injured*, he stayed in the game.	1	( )
10. He answered *in order that you might know the truth*.		( )

Place R if right; W, if wrong:

	W	
11. He will tell us when it is noon that we can not go.	W	( )
12. In spite of all the mean things he has said.	R	( )
13. He asked me, "Who did it?"	W	( )
14. The just man fears no law.	R	( )
15. When tired of arguing, pick up a book.		( )

AFTER MASTERY, TURN TO PAGE 62

Number wrong ____

Hints: Restrictive & Nonrestrictive Modifiers

37.0 There are two kinds of modifiers—restrictive and nonrestrictive. The restrictive modifier is necessary for a correct understanding of the sentence; the nonrestrictive may be omitted and the main meaning of the sentence is still clear:
> Restrictive: The man who telephoned you is my neighbor.
> Nonrestrictive: John Jones, the man who telephoned you, is my neighbor.

37.1 The restrictive adjective clause points out and identifies the noun or pronoun it modifies; in other words, it restricts its meaning. If this clause is omitted, the sense of the sentence is changed or lost. It is important to note that this clause is *not* set off by commas.
> Examples: The man *who hesitates* is lost.
> The tree *which bore the largest fruit* is a pear tree.
> This is the house *that Jack built.*

37.2 The nonrestrictive adjective clause supplies additional information but is not necessary to point out or identify the meaning of the noun or pronoun it modifies. It should be set off by commas, which you may think of as "lifting handles." If an adjective clause can be lifted out without losing the meaning, you can be sure it is nonrestrictive.
> Examples: The teacher, *who used to play professional football,* likes sports.
> This book, *which you should read,* has an interesting plot.
> Jim Jones, *who is a senior,* spoke to the assembly.

37.3 Adverbial clauses, as well as adjective clauses, may be restrictive or nonrestrictive. Usually the adverbial clause at the beginning of a sentence is nonrestrictive, and is separated from the rest of the sentence by a comma.
> Restrictive: We shall come *when you call us.*
> Nonrestrictive: *Although you may not want us,* we shall come.

37.4 Participial phrases may be restrictive or nonrestrictive. It should be remembered that the nonrestrictive participial phrase is set off by commas:
> Nonrestrictive: *Having won the game,* our team celebrated the victory.
> Restrictive: The lady *smiling at me* is my wife.

Hint 37. Enclose nonrestrictive modifiers with commas

NOW WORK EXERCISE 27

Exercise 27

Trial I — Place in the proper parentheses R if the modifier is restrictive and N if it is nonrestrictive:

		Right answers for page 61	Your answers for page 63
1.	The boy *sitting on the porch* is my son.	2	( )
2.	The horse *which won the race* was a bay.	2	( )
3.	*Sitting on the bench,* the men discussed politics.	2	( )
4.	Jim Jones, *our policeman,* is six feet tall.	1	( )
5.	George Washington, *who was our first president,* slept here.		( )
6.	The price *that he paid* was low.		( )
7.	The price, *which he paid gladly,* was low.	2	( )
8.	He *that pays the piper* picks the tune.	1	( )
		3	

Place R if right; W, if wrong: 1

9.	Men, who falter, seldom achieve greatness.		( )
10.	This house which Jack built is expensive.		( )
11.	You are the one, whom I called.	2	( )
12.	Students who rarely study often fail.	5	( )
13.	The boy while reaching for the fruit, fell and broke his leg.		( )
14.	When the challenge comes, you must face the issue.		( )
15.	Modifiers that are restrictive should not be set off by commas.	W	( )

CHECK your answers with the right ones on page 65. If you miss none, go ahead. If you miss one or more, try

R
W
R

Number wrong

Trial II — IDENTIFY as in Trial I: W

1.	Six beautiful girls, *singing carols,* knocked at my door.		( )
2.	He will go *when the clock strikes four.*		( )
3.	*Hoping you are willing,* we ask you for help.		( )
4.	The poem *which he wrote* was mournful.		( )
5.	This city, *which I often visit,* is famous for tourists.	2	( )
6.	This city *which I visited* is famous for tourists.	1	( )
7.	Any person *causing trouble* will be arrested.	2	( )
8.	The girl *playing the piano* is my cousin.	2	( )

Place R if right; W, if wrong:

3
2

9.	Columbus, which is my home town, is a pretty city.	1	( )
10.	When the band starts playing, stand up and shout.	1	( )
11.	This story which you have heard before is true.	3	( )
12.	I can not leave until the boss comes back.	3	( )
13.	This is the house, where he lived.		( )
14.	If sufficiently heated, iron melts.		( )
15.	This is the saddest story, which I have ever heard.		( )

AFTER MASTERY, TURN TO PAGE 64

W
W
R
R
R

Number wrong

Review   Grammar

Just to make assurance doubly sure, are you willing to take a test again?

If so, review all errors and difficulties since the last test.

Grade yourself on your first attempt, using the previous scale. You will recall it looks like this:

ERRORS	GRADE
0 - 2	A
3 - 4	B
5 - 6	C
7 - 8	D
More than 8	F, or failed

If you make an A or even a B, you are making good progress. If your grade is C or lower, organize a systematic review so you can be sure of mastery.

Note the right answers in the Key on page 67 and references to the Hints for each item missed.

FORWARD! ATTACK!
(It would please me if you made an A!)

Review Test IV

Review Test IV A. IDENTIFY by appropriate number the italicized words (1. participle; 2. gerund; 3. infinitive):

		Right answers for page 63	Your answers for page 65

1. There was an argument concerning his *departing*. R ( )
2. He had a great desire *to fly*. R ( )
3. He heard her *talking* to him. N ( )

N
N

B. Mark A if active voice; P, if passive:

4. *Hoping* for the best, he drove away. R ( )
5. *Being recognized*, he made a bow. N ( )
6. *Having been discovered*, the enemy ran. R ( )

C. Mark usage in sentence according to this code: 1. subject; 2. object; 3. object of a preposition; 4. subjective complement.

7. His intention is *to fight him*. W ( )
8. *His running away* worried his mother. W ( )
9. She objected *to my purchasing expensive gifts*. W ( )

R
W

D. Place R if the italicized clause is restrictive; U, if unrestrictive:

10. This is the house *that Jack built*. R ( )
11. Two soldiers, *who were loitering there*, came to her rescue. R ( )
12. John Smith, *who lives next door to me*, is a good neighbor. ( )
13. The John Smith *who wrote this letter* is not the one I know. ( )
14. The pig *that squeals loudest* gets help. ( )
15. My pig, *which weighs 200 pounds*, is fat and saucy. ( )

E. Place R if right; W, if wrong:

16. His standing in the aisle attracted attention. N ( )
17. Reaching for my hat, the monkey was found wearing it. R ( )
18. They agree this very morning to buy tickets. N ( )
19. Returning to the site of the dreadful crime. R ( )
20. Generally speaking, English spelling is difficult. N ( )
21. I heard him talking to his mother. N ( )
22. A woman who talks too much is shunned. R ( )
23. Who did he take her to be? R ( )
24. We were pleased at his returning so promptly. ( )
25. Him entering the room caused a sensation. ( )
26. He demanded to as soon as possible receive the money. ( )
27. They made him answer the letter. R ( )
28. Busily engaged in eating peanuts, the lady looked at the elephant. R ( )
29. While working this morning, the whistle blew three times. W ( )
30. I hate to tell again a tale once fully told. R ( )

AFTER MASTERY, TURN TO PAGE 66

W
R
W

_____
Number Wrong

Grade_____

[65]

Hints: Comparison — Grammar

38.0 Adjectives and adverbs have three forms to show variation of degree in quality, quantity, or manner. These three forms are the *positive,* the *comparative,* and the *superlative* degree.

38.1 The positive degree is the basic degree, stating merely a quality, quantity, or manner, and shows no comparison.
> Examples: She is a *pleasant* lady. He ran a *swift* race.

38.2 The comparative degree shows comparison or relationship between two objects. It may be formed in three ways: 1. adding *er* to the positive form; 2. using adverbial modifiers, *more* for an upward comparison, *less* for a downward comparison; 3. irregularly, by changing the word.
> Example: This candy is *sweeter.* He is *better.* He is *taller* than I. He is *more eloquent* than his brother. She is *less talented* than her sister. This is *worse.*

38.3 The superlative degree shows comparison or relationship among three or more objects. It may be formed in three ways: 1. adding *est* to the positive form; 2. using adverbial modifiers *most* and *least;* 3. irregularly, by changing the word.
> Example: She is *good.* He is *better.* John is *best.*
> This candy is *sweet.* Yours is *sweeter.* His is *sweetest.*
> This happens *more often;* that happens *most often.*

Hint 38. Do not use the superlative degree when comparing only two objects.
It is proper to use the comparative degree when comparing two objects, and the superlative degree when comparing three or more objects.
> Wrong: Give me the *best* of these two.
> Right: Give me the *better* of these two.
> Right: He is the *taller* of the two sons, and she is the *shorter* of the two daughters.
> Right: Select the *best* of these four citizens. He was the *poorest* of all the players.

39.0 Double comparatives and superlatives are errors. Sometimes we are tricked into using *more* or *most* before a modifier that is already in the comparative or superlative form. This attempt at emphasis is incorrect:
> Wrong: He is *more brainier* than his sister.
> Wrong: He is *less handsomer* too.
> Wrong: She is the *most sweetest* singer I have ever heard.
> Wrong: This was the *most unkindest* cut of all.

Hint 39. Avoid the double comparative or the double superlative

NOW WORK THE EXERCISE ON PAGE 67

Exercise 28

		Right answers for page 65	Your answers for page 67
Trial I	Place R if right; W, if wrong:		
1.	This is the tallest of the twins.	2–30.12	( )
2.	This is the more expensiver car.	3–30.13	( )
3.	This game was worser than the other.	1–30.11	( )
4.	He did the mostest with the leastest.		( )
5.	She done badder than me.		( )
6.	John is more greedier than Jim.	A–31.1	( )
7.	This is the farthest of these two towns.	P–31.1	( )
8.	She is the more beautiful of her three sisters.	P–31.1	( )
9.	This is the most homeliest dress of the lot.		( )
10.	It is badder than I thought.		( )
11.	Use the dictionary more oftener.		( )
12.	Of the two teams, ours is the best.	4–32.0	( )
13.	The gooder you try to be, the more disappointeder you are.	1–31.3	( )
14.	Of Jim and me, he did the least.	3–31.2	( )
15.	You are more stupider than I am.		( )

CHECK your answers with the right ones on page 69. If you miss none, go ahead. If you miss one or more, try

			Number wrong
		R–37.1	
		U–37.2	
		U–37.2	
Trial II	Place R if right; W, if wrong:	R–37.1	
		R–37.1	
1.	Your theme was longer than last week's.	U–37.2	( )
2.	She is the dearest teacher I know.		( )
3.	I'll take the better of these two melons.		( )
4.	She is the best singer in the chorus.	R–31	( )
5.	Do come more often.	W–33	( )
6.	It happened in the least of all these cities.	W–34.4	( )
7.	He does his work least carefully of all the class.	W–30	( )
8.	Less hilarity, please!	R–35.15	( )
9.	He entered the room more quietly than did his sister.	R–31.3	( )
10.	I picked the worst apple in the sack.	R–37.1	( )
11.	You are dearer to me than she is.	W–32.1	( )
12.	Of all contributors he gave the most.	R–31.3	( )
13.	Vote for the better of these two men.	W–31.3	( )
14.	My wife was the prettiest woman there!	W–32	( )
15.	May the poorer team lose!	R–32.0	( )

AFTER MASTERY, TURN TO PAGE 68

W–33	
W–34.3	Number wrong
R–32.0	

Hints: Illogical Comparisons — Grammar

40.0 Some adjectives and adverbs are logically incapable of comparison. Such words are *absolute, fatal, impossible, perfect, unique, dead, final,* etc. To avoid this error of illogical comparison, it is good practice to drop the sign of comparison or to use qualifying adverbs such as *nearly* and *almost*:

    Wrong: This was the *most* unique feature.
    Right: This was the unique feature.
    Wrong: This was the *most* fatal wound.
    Right: This was the fatal wound.
    Right: This was *almost* impossible.

Hint 40. Avoid comparing modifiers whose meaning does not permit comparison

41.0 If we wish to be logical, we must be sure whether the object compared stands by itself or is a member of the total membership of the class. The problem really reduces to the question whether *other* should be included or omitted:

    Wrong: Jane is a prettier girl than any in her class.
    Right: Jane is a prettier girl than any *other* in her class.
    Wrong: Jim is better than any member of his team.
    Right: Jim is better than any *other* member of his team.

Hint 41. Avoid comparing a thing with itself.

42.0 Confusion also arises if the writer tries to include two comparisons in the same statement. Sometimes the correction produces an awkward, difficult construction. In such cases it is best to revise the original sentence so the double comparison is clear and the result a smooth statement:

    Wrong: John is as sure if not surer than Mary.
    Right: John is as sure as, if not surer than, Mary. (Awkward!)
    Right: John is as sure as Mary, if not surer than she.

Hint 42. Include all words necessary for a proper comparison.

43.0 We can not strengthen our comparatives and superlatives in modern English by doubling the comparatives or superlatives. This is particularly true of the Double Negative:

    Wrong: I *can't hardly* speak.
    Right: I can *hardly* speak.
    Wrong: He *don't* know *nothing*.
    Right: He *doesn't* know anything.
    Right: His gift was *not unwelcome*. (Here two negatives form a modest affirmative. This type of usage is called *litotes,* and is an approved type of emphasis by understatement.)

Hint 43. Avoid confusing and improper double negatives.

NOW WORK EXERCISE 29

Exercise 29

	Right answers for page 67	Your answers for page 69

Trial I   Place R if right; W, if wrong:

1. This is the most unique feature of the book.   W   ( )
2. I am a citizen of no mean city.   W   ( )
3. He don't know no better.   W   ( )
4. He is stronger than any man on his team.   W   ( )
5. John does as well if not better than Jack.   W   ( )
6. Solomon was the wisest of all kings.   W   ( )
7. London is larger than any city in England.   W   ( )
8. Cursing is the most inexcusable of all the other vices.   W   ( )
9. This is the more preferable form.   W   ( )
10. The Ohio River flows faster in spring than in fall.   W   ( )
11. This examination was longer than the one last year.   W   ( )
12. The younger of the three brothers is the brighter.   W   ( )
13. We ain't heard nothing.   W   ( )
14. He speaks better than any other boy in his class.   W   ( )
15. Of all the texts which I have examined, this is the best.   W   ( )

CHECK your answers with the right ones on page 71. If you miss none, go ahead. If you miss one or more, try

Number wrong

Trial II   Place R if right; W, if wrong:

1. We ain't got nothin' but cornbread.   R   ( )
2. I can't scarcely talk.   R   ( )
3. He is the oldest of the children.   R   ( )
4. This was the most perfect poem.   R   ( )
5. He is as sturdy if not sturdier than his older brother.   R   ( )
6. It is a most remarkable play.   R   ( )
7. Her precision is nearly absolute.   R   ( )
8. Her smile was not unpleasant.   R   ( )
9. The taller of the three brothers is the leader.   R   ( )
10. John is abler than any man in his class.   R   ( )
11. You wouldn't hardly act so.   R   ( )
12. He is the mightiest of mankind.   R   ( )
13. My love is brighter than the stars.   R   ( )
14. She isn't allowed to go nowhere.   R   ( )
15. I say, "The longer, the better."   R   ( )

AFTER MASTERY, TURN TO PAGE 70

Number wrong

Hints: Coordinating Conjunctions Grammar

44.0 A conjunction is a word used to join words, phrases, or clauses. Sometimes, for the sake of coherence, it may connect sentences. Its function is to join two or more parts. There are two main groups—coordinating conjunctions and subordinating conjunctions.

44.1 A coordinating conjunction connects parts of equal rank. There are three kinds—simple conjunctions, correlative conjunctions, and conjunctive adverbs.

    44.11 The simple conjunction is usually a single word such as *and, but, or, nor,* and *for:*
        Connecting words: You *and* I went.
        Connecting phrases: It was red in the middle *and* on top.
        Connecting clauses: He smiled *and* then he walked away.

    44.12 Correlative conjunctions are used in pairs. Most frequently used are *both, and; either, or; neither, nor; not only, but also:*
        Both you *and* he assented. *Neither* John *nor* Jim knew the answer.

    44.13 Conjunctive adverbs are adverbs used to join main clauses. They have the dual nature of conjunction and adverb. They can not join subordinate clauses. Some common ones are *however, thus, besides, still, also, for example, therefore, nevertheless:*
        He did not answer; *however,* we decided to go ahead.
        He plays the piano; *besides,* he sings beautifully.

44.2 A conjunction should not be used needlessly nor carelessly. Each serves its particular purpose and should be selected with precision.
    Wrong: I will try *and* do better next time.
    Right: I will try to do better next time.
    Wrong: No one can deny *but* he has influence.
    Right: No one can deny that he has influence.
    Wrong: She was angry *and* she smiled.
    Right: She was angry *but* she smiled.

44.3 Correlative conjunctions should not dangle, squint, or be misplaced. They are used in pairs, and each member of the pair should be followed by the same grammatical structure. This sameness is called *parallelism.* They should be used to relate two ideas, not more than two:
    Wrong: Chicago is *neither* the biggest *or* the most beautiful city in America.
    Right: Chicago is *neither* the biggest *nor* the most beautiful city in America.
    Wrong: He *not only* gave me advice *but also* aid.
    Right: He gave me *not only* advice *but also* aid.
    Wrong: The play was not *either* strange *nor* exciting.
    Right: The play was *neither* strange *nor* exciting.

Hint 44. Be precise in your choice and use of coordinating conjunctions.

NOW WORK EXERCISE 30.

Exercise 30

		Right answers for page 69	Your answers for page 71
Trial I	Place R if right; W, if wrong:		
1.	Neither Jack or Jill could climb it.	W	( )
2.	He not only called me names but he also hit me.	R	( )
3.	Both Jim, Jack, and Harry are college graduates.	W	( )
4.	I wanted to go and I had no money.	W	( )
5.	Who doubts but that Shakespeare lived.	W	( )
6.	Give me neither poverty nor riches.	R	( )
7.	He was neither rich nor poor.	W	( )
8.	She dressed not only richly but tactfully.	W	( )
9.	A harrow is drawn over the field and which covers the seed.	W	( )
10.	We must cut expenses or our funds will vanish.	R	( )
11.	He knew better but he answered.	R	( )
12.	Try and call me early.	W	( )
13.	He ran away; thus he ended our relationship.	W	( )
14.	The colors of the flag are red, white, and blue.	R	( )
15.	Time and tide wait for no man.	R	( )

CHECK your answers with the right ones on page 73. If you miss none, go ahead. If you miss one or more, try

Number wrong

Trial II	Place R if right; W, if wrong:		
1.	The game was not either exciting nor well executed.	W	( )
2.	He gave me neither help nor hope.	W	( )
3.	She will try and take the English test.	R	( )
4.	Conjunctions may join words; for example, *but* is such a word.	W	( )
5.	He refused to contribute; nevertheless, the project will prosper.	W	( )
6.	Both John and I and Jim took the test.	R	( )
7.	She was happy and she didn't show it.	R	( )
8.	He not only wanted my money but also my job.	R	( )
9.	Either you or I could answer him.	W	( )
10.	Neither the teacher or the pupil knew the answer.	W	( )
11.	He does not study; however, he gets good grades.	W	( )
12.	You must admit that neither Jack or Jill did it.	R	( )
13.	Both you and I went.	R	( )
14.	He avoided the teacher, for he knew the teacher had given him a low grade.	W	( )
15.	We cannot go; neither can we stay here.	R	( )

AFTER MASTERY, TURN TO PAGE 72

Number wrong

Hints: Subordinating Conjunctions Grammar

45.0 A subordinating conjunction introduces a subordinate (or dependent) clause. It connects a dependent clause to a main clause. This dependent clause is either a noun or an adverbial clause, as the adjective clause uses the relative pronouns. Some of the important subordinate conjunctions are *if, since, although, unless, when, where, as if, even though, in order that, because, as.*
> It came *when* we least expected it.
> I know *because* you told me.
> *Unless* you return my tools, I can not work.

45.1 The relative pronoun acts as a subordinating conjunction in connecting an adjective clause to a noun or pronoun. Common relative pronouns are *who, which,* and *that. Who* is used for persons; *which* is used for things; and *that,* for either:
> He is the man *who* knows it all.
> This is the train *which* you should take.
> This is the house *that* Jack built.

Hint 45. Be precise in your choice and use of subordinating conjunctions.
> Wrong: *Being as how I went,* I should pay my share.
> Right: *Because* I went, I should pay my share.
> Wrong: I read *where* he had died.
> Right: I read *that* he had died.

45.2 *So* is correctly used as a conjunctive adverb with a semicolon preceding it, but it is often overused and misused. In fact, *so* often is a trap for the *comma splice.* To avoid excessive use, substitute *therefore, thus, accordingly* (with a semicolon preceding), or rephrase the sentence.
> Wrong: He had to work, so he went early.
> Right: He had to work; so he went early.
> Wrong: He failed, so he took the course again;
> Right: He failed; therefore he took the course again.

46.0 *Like* is commonly misused for *as if. Like* may be used as a noun, a verb, or a preposition, but its use as a conjunction is too colloquial for formal use. *Like* as a preposition should introduce a phrase; it should not be used to introduce a clause. (Here we regretfully admit that more and more good people disobey this injunction. We advise that you stick by us and this book.)

Hint 46. Avoid using like as a conjunction.
> As noun: His *like* we rarely see. As verb: I *like* you. As conjunction: (Wrong) Do *like* he said.
> Right: Do *as* he said. As preposition: He looks *like* his mother.
> Wrong: He ran *like* he could run forever.
> Right: He ran *as if* he could run forever.

Exercise 31

	Right answers for page 71	Your answers for page 73

Trial I   Place R if right; W, if wrong:

1. He was so rushed until I came. — W ( )
2. I came when he called me. — R ( )
3. He acted like he hated me. — W ( )
4. Do as you wish. — W ( )
5. He had to study; so he did not go. — W ( )
6. I heard where he had died. — R ( )
7. He helped me; therefore, I paid him. — R ( )
8. I like him because he looks like me. — R ( )
9. She wanted him to call, so she wrote him. — W ( )
10. He worked so that he could go to school. — R ( )
11. The reason he went is because he wanted to. — R ( )
12. I wished I'd done like he did. — W ( )
13. When Duty calls, the youth replies. — R ( )
14. She asked him to call her, so he did. — R ( )
15. I answered like he told me to. — R ( )

Number wrong _____

CHECK your answers with the right ones on page 75. If you miss none, go ahead. If you miss one or more, try

Trial II   Place R if right; W, if wrong:

1. Do like I told you. — W ( )
2. He knows you, so you should ask him. — R ( )
3. He promised to come; so he arrived at dawn. — W ( )
4. That is the man which knocked at my door. — R ( )
5. I like his like of man. — R ( )
6. I heard where he had done wrong. — W ( )
7. Beings as I'm tired, will you go? — W ( )
8. It tastes like a cigarette should! — W ( )
9. I wish I could be like him. — R ( )
10. He acted as if he would finish. — W ( )
11. Six o'clock is when you come. — R ( )
12. I read where he had gone away. — W ( )
13. I cried, so she kissed me. — R ( )
14. This is the runner that defeated all others. — R ( )
15. I concur, although I have my doubts. — R ( )

AFTER MASTERY, TURN TO PAGE 74

Number wrong _____

[73]

Hints: Prepositions and Interjections Gramma

47.0   A preposition shows the relationship of a noun or pronoun to some other word in the sentence. It takes an object; the preposition with its object forms a prepositional phrase. There are at least seventy prepositions in English, some of the simpler being *at, by, for, in, like,* and *to.* Usually the preposition precedes its object, but sometimes it follows: Whom did you give it *to*?
It may appear even at the end of a sentence. This usage led to the satirical rule that "a preposition is a poor word to end a sentence with." Sir Winston Churchill's famous reply to this principle was, "This is the kind of thing up with which I don't intend to put."
However, the preposition presents its own serious problems in its peculiar idiomatic uses. (An idiom is the result of custom in language and may not be logically grammatical.) Just a few of these idomatic uses are the following: guard *against*; profit *by;* adept *in;* agree *to* a thing, but agree *with* a person; angry *at* a thing, but angry *with* a person; concern *in* (interest), concern *for* (troubled), concern *with* (a person); etc.

47.1   The object of a preposition is always in the objective case. It is easy to err if the preposition has two or more objects:
        Wrong: He gave it to him and I.
        Right: He gave it to him and me.
        Wrong: She told the story to he and I.
        Right: She told the story to him and me.

Hint 47. Place all objects of a preposition in the objective case.

47.2   Prepositions are important and should not be omitted even in complex structures; neither should they be used needlessly:
        Wrong: He is worthy our help.
        Right: He is worthy *of* our help.
        Wrong: He has neither respect nor faith in his teacher.
        Right: He has neither respect *for* nor faith in his teacher.

Hint 48. Do not omit prepositions when they are needed nor use them needlessly.
        Wrong: *In* what state is Toledo *in*?
        Right: In what state is Toledo?
        Wrong: He fell off *of* the wagon.
        Right: He fell off the wagon.

49.0   The interjection expresses strong feeling or emotion. It has no grammatical connection with the sentence. Occasional interjections may be necessary, but overuse is not good style. The interjection is followed by the exclamation point or the comma, depending on the strength of the emotion.

Hint 49. Do not overuse the interjection.
        Right: Oh, what shall I do! (*Oh* usually stands alone)
        Right: O Judge, great is thy fame! (*O* usually used with another word)

NOW WORK EXERCISE 32

Exercise 32

Trial I Place R if right; W, if wrong:

		Right answers for page 73	Your answers for page 75
1.	He stays to home.	W	( )
2.	Hurrah! Our flag is still waving!	R	( )
3.	He came in for to see me.	W	( )
4.	Of what is water composed of?	R	( )
5.	This, alas, is all I know.	R	( )
6.	He was prevented going.	W	( )
7.	O Sea, what mysteries thou hidest!	R	( )
8.	This requires a curiosity and a love of meeting people.	R	( )
9.	He fell in the cistern.	W	( )
10.	The two sisters quarreled among each other.	R	( )
11.	He walked into the cave.	W	( )
12.	Between the three of us, it should remain a secret.	W	( )
13.	Over the fence is out.	R	( )
14.	This book is different and more costly than the other.	W	( )
15.	Pshaw! You know better than that!	W	( )

CHECK your answers with the right ones on page 77. If you missed none, go ahead. If you missed one or more, try

Number wrong ____

Trial II Check R if right; W, if wrong:

1.	Oh City of my dreams, welcome us.	W	( )
2.	From his boat he fell in the water.	W	( )
3.	Please be kind to he and I.	R	( )
4.	Between us three, what is best to do?	W	( )
5.	Farewell! A long farewell to all my greatness!	R	( )
6.	Hush! What noise is this?	W	( )
7.	Quick! We must hasten.	W	( )
8.	It looked like he would win.	W	( )
9.	He stood above Jim, Jack, and I.	R	( )
10.	This requires a love and interest in music.	R	( )
11.	Dear me! This is too sad!	W	( )
12.	Hark, hark! the lark at heaven's gate sings.	W	( )
13.	For what did he come for?	W	( )
14.	He fell off of the porch.	R	( )
15.	Who did he come for?	R	( )

AFTER MASTERY, TURN TO PAGE 76

Number wrong ____

Hints: Sentence Style — Grammar

50.0   Clear sentences indicate clear thought. A well-written sentence should have unity, coherence, and emphasis; in other words, it has unity if it treats one topic; it has coherence if the parts hold together; and it has emphasis if important parts stand out as important parts.
We now present a few simple principles that are basic to good style:

Hint 50. Vary your sentence structure.
Robert Louis Stevenson said of writing, "Be infinitely various."

50.1   Vary length. Do not use only long sentences. An editor of a famous newspaper insisted that his cub reporters limit the length of their sentences to seventeen words. Do not use a succession of short sentences: this fault is called "primer style." Study good prose to note how authors vary length.

50.2   Vary type of sentence. Remember as far as clauses are concerned, you have for your choosing the simple, the compound, the complex, and the compound-complex sentence. As far as purpose is concerned, you have the declarative, the interrogative, the imperative, and the exclamatory. As far as arrangement of parts is concerned, you have these three available types: (1) the loose sentence, in which meaning is clear before the end is reached; (2) the balanced sentence, in which similar or opposing thoughts have similar structure; and (3) the periodic, in which the parts are so arranged that the meaning is not clear before the end of the sentence.

    Loose: He came to my house early in the morning.
    Balanced: To err is human; to forgive, divine.
    Periodic: If you must insult me, if you must refuse my offer, then there remains only this — go!

50.3   Use the triple construction. Good writers like to use parts in three's — three adjectives, three phrases, three clauses. In a triple construction, let the last construction be longest or heaviest: I came, I saw, I conquered (three clauses). She was tall, gentle, and beautiful (three adjectives). He was first in war, first in peace, and first in the hearts of his countrymen (three phrases).

50.4   Use parallel structure. In parallelism, like ideas are in like structure — a balance or a series of nouns, of infinitives, of subordinate clauses, of main clauses.

    Wrong: I like golf, to swim, skating.
    Right: I like golfing, swimming, skating (all gerunds).
    Wrong: I told him to dress more neatly and that he should polish his shoes.
    Right: I told him that he should dress more neatly and that he should polish his shoes (clauses).

50.5   Prefer the active voice. It is better to say, *John hit a home run* than to say *A home run was hit by John*.

50.6   Occasionally venture a fresh figure of speech.

    Simile: His flight was like a jet's. My love is like a melody.
    Metaphor: Night's candles are burnt out. Hitch your wagon to a star.

NOW TRY EXERCISE 33

Exercise 33

Trial I   IDENTIFY structure by placing in the parentheses the proper symbol (TC, proper triple construction; PS, primer style; PV, weak use of passive voice; LP, lack of parallelism; BS, balanced sentence):

#	Sentence	Right answers for page 75	Your answers for page 77
1.	He likes dramatics and to play in the orchestra.	W	( )
2.	I went to town. I bought a pole. I found some bait. I went fishing.	R	( )
3.	"... nobly planned, to warn, to comfort, and command."	W	( )
4.	His intentions were asked about by her father.	W	( )
5.	A book is pleasant to read and it gives you facts.	R	( )
6.	He came directly, at great speed, and without making a noise.	W	( )
7.	This neighbor was a sportsman, a scholar, and a gentleman.	R	( )
8.	He sees too clearly to be vague; he is too serious to be fickle.	W	( )
9.	The pretty girl was smiled at by the cadets.	W	( )
10.	He reads. He studies. He never misses classes. He likes school.	W	( )
11.	Our hero is a tall, strong, handsome man.	R	( )
12.	Our forces are superior in the air and when they sail the sea.	W	( )
13.	It is too strenuous to play ball and then you have to study.	R	( )
14.	He had a lean look and he also seemed hungry.	W	( )
15.	The lady advanced, smiled, and spoke gently to the child.	R	( )

CHECK your answers with the right ones on page 79. If you have missed none, go ahead. If you miss one or more, try

Number wrong

Trial II   USE the same directions given for Trial I:

#	Sentence	Right	Your
1.	In the morning I work; in the afternoon I study.	W	( )
2.	I came, I saw, I conquered.	W	( )
3.	He asked me to reply and then I should come to him.	W	( )
4.	I went. I saw him. He ran. I followed. I lost him.	W	( )
5.	I found out his name, James Jones, and that his interest was playing cards.	R	( )
6.	She is tall, gracious, and queenly.	R	( )
7.	He likes boating, to ski, and he skates in the winter time.	R	( )
8.	It was reported that the game was won by us.	W	( )
9.	The sequence of events has been previously related by me.	W	( )
10.	His manners we admire; his character we abhor.	W	( )
11.	I bought food, appliances, and clothing.	R	( )
12.	He likes apples, I do too. Mary does not. Helen does.	R	( )
13.	Her mother taught her to be courteous, gentle, and ladylike.	W	( )
14.	Where law ends, tyranny begins.	W	( )
15.	Books are friends, neighbors, teachers.	W	( )

AFTER MASTERY, TURN TO PAGE 78

Number wrong

Review   Grammar

Yes, that time has come again!

Review all errors and difficulties since the last test.

Grade yourself on your first attempt, using our scale. You will recall it looks like this:

ERRORS	GRADE
0 - 2	A
3 - 4	B
5 - 6	C
7 - 8	D
More than 8	F, or failed

If you make an A or even a B, you are making good progress. If your grade is C or lower, organize a systematic review so you can be sure of mastery. Note the right answer in the Key on page 81 and references to the Hints for each item missed.

NOW, BOLDLY AND BRAVELY TRY THE TEST!
(I am rooting for you! I hope you make an A!)

Review Test V

Review Test V Place R if right; W, if wrong:

		Right answers for page 77	Your answers for page 79
1.	She is the shorter of the two sisters.	LP	( )
2.	This is the most oftenest error.	PS	( )
3.	This dog is the larger of the three animals.	TC	( )
4.	Jim is brighter than any other member of his class.	PV	( )
5.	This was the most perfect act I have ever seen.	LP	( )
6.	I am a citizen of no mean city.	LP	( )
7.	I can't hardly speak above a whisper.	TC	( )
8.	Jane is the prettiest of all the girls.	BS	( )
9.	He ain't got nothing.	PV	( )
10.	She was unhappy, but she answered.	PS	( )
11.	He did not reply; however, we decided to go.	TC	( )
12.	He not only gave me help but also encouraged me.	LP	( )
13.	His action was not either strange or queer.	LP	( )
14.	Give me neither poverty nor riches.	LP	( )
15.	She will try and get the money.	TC	( )
16.	He offered the flowers to Jane and me.		( )
17.	He has neither love or hope in mortals.		( )
18.	I read where he had gone to Alaska.		( )
19.	He had to get up early; so he used an alarm clock.		( )
20.	This is the car who did the damage.		( )
21.	I came. She went. He knocked. I did too. Then we yelled.		( )
22.	He loves to dance, swimming, and that he may sleep late.	BS	( )
23.	He acted like he wanted to return.	TC	( )

Identify the italicized parts by placing appropriate numbers in the parentheses (1. triple construction; 2. balanced sentence; 3. parallelism; 4. periodic sentence; 5. figure of speech):

		LP	
		PS	
		LP	
		TC	
		LP	
24.	His reaction was as sweet as a maiden's kiss.	PV	( )
25.	He pushed forward with faith, hope, and prayer.	PV	( )
26.	When all is said and done, our best hopes depend on him.	BS	( )
27.	Do unto others as you would have others do unto you.	TC	( )
28.	Night's candles are burnt out.	PS	( )
29.	The coward hesitates to act; the hero dares to do.	TC	( )
30.	He offered us only blood, sweat, and tears.	BS	( )
		TC	

AFTER MASTERY, TURN TO PAGE 80

Number wrong _____

Grade _____

Hints: End Punctuation – The Period

51.0 Punctuation consists in the use of marks to make clear the meaning of written language. Some of its rules are arbitrary; others are controlled by the writer for rhetorical purposes. The modern viewpoint is to reduce or simplify the amount of punctuation.

Hint 51. When in doubt whether or not to punctuate, don't!
51.1 In general it may be said that punctuation may be used
    51.11 to end or terminate a statement (use period; question mark; exclamation point);
    51.12 to introduce a statement (use comma; colon; or dash);
    51.13 to separate parts (use comma; semicolon; dash; hyphen; or apostrophe);
    51.14 to enclose parts (commas; dashes; quotation marks; parentheses; brackets. These should be used in pairs).
51.2 Punctuation marks differ in strength of stress. Thus, the period as a mark of ending is stronger than the semicolon, which, in turn, is stronger than the comma. The comma is the weakest of the three. The error called the comma splice is due to the fact that the writer feels the comma is as strong as the semicolon or period. In like manner, dashes or parentheses are stronger than commas in parenthetical material.

Hint 52. Use the period as a strong terminal point.
52.1 Use the period after a declarative sentence: Truth crushed to earth shall rise again.
52.2 Use the period after a weak imperative sentence: Please pass the butter.
52.3 Use the period after an indirect question: He asked me whether or not you would go.
52.4 Use the period after a proper elliptical statement: Did you do it? Yes. (The elliptical expression must not be an improper fragment)

Hint 53. Use the period after most abbreviations.
53.1 If the abbreviation appears at the end of the sentence, do not use two periods: He came at 6 a.m.
53.2 If the abbreviation appears within the sentence, the abbreviation period is followed by any mark of punctuation which would be usually proper: He came at 6 a. m.; then we ate breakfast.
Other examples: Mr.; Mrs.; i.e.; M. D.; ff.; lbs.; a. m. (or A. M.); etc.
53.2 In an outline, place a period after every symbol such as Roman numerals, letters, and Arabic numerals, but do not place a period at the ends of lines in a topical outline.

NOW WORK THE EXERCISE ON PAGE 81

Exercise 34

		Right answers for page 79	Your answers for page 81
Trial I	Place R if right: W, if wrong:		

		Right answers for page 79	Your answers for page 81
1.	Everyone did his best.	R—38.2	( )
2.	Please give me the book.	W—39.0	( )
3.	He told me that he never studied.	W—38.2	( )
4.	No. You know better than to ask me.	R—41.0	( )
5.	Let us all go to town?	W—40.0	( )
6.	The scenery being very beautiful.	R—43	( )
7.	This is a delightful book for young people.	W—43	( )
8.	He answered incorrectly, he did not know the answer.	R—41.0	( )
9.	He informed the judge that Jim had done it.	W—43	( )
10.	He said that I should ask him?	R—44.2	( )
11.	Let's climb to the top, the view is very beautiful.	R—44.13	( )
12.	Yes. I am ready. All aboard!	R—44.3	( )
13.	John Smith, M. D. (b. 1910; d. 1964), wrote this article for a medical journal.	W—44.3	( )
14.	He asked him whether or not I should go?	R—44.12	( )
15.	Please come to our picnic.	W—44.2	( )
		R—47.1	

CHECK your answers with the right ones on page 83. If you have missed none, go ahead. If you have missed one or more, try

W—44.12
W—45
R—45.2

Number wrong

Trial II	Place R if right; W, if wrong:	W—45.1	
		W—50.1	
1.	He bought candy, fruit, and etc.	W—50.4	( )
2.	He wondered if you would sing?	W—46	( )
3.	No. I do not intend to pay that bill.		( )
4.	Wisdom is better than rubies.		( )
5.	He then refused my offer, I knew he would.		( )
6.	Please pass the cream and sugar!		( )
7.	Will you come at 9 a. m.?		( )
8.	God helps them that help themselves.	5—50.6	( )
9.	He asked me if you would buy one?	1—50.3	( )
10.	Mr. and Mrs. Jim Jones came at 8 p. m.	4—50.2	( )
11.	He never tried to answer me, he did not wish to come.	2—50.2	( )
12.	Good books are good friends.	5—50.6	( )
13.	Will you go? Certainly.	2—50.2	( )
14.	He asked him whether or not he could play?	1—50.3	( )
15.	As the twig is bent, the tree is inclined.		( )

AFTER MASTERY, TURN TO PAGE 82

Number wrong

Hints: Various Uses for the Period — Punctuation

54.0 Most abbreviations take the period. But usage has produced some exceptions:
Do not use the period after

54.10 Nicknames: Pat, Ed, Al, Gert, Joe;
54.11 Radio and television stations: WBNC, CBS, ABC, WRCA;
54.12 National or international agencies: WAC, UN, NATO, CIO;
54.13 Often-used abbreviations: gym, dorm, math, exam;
54.14 The ordinal numbers: 1st, 2nd, 3rd, 4th;
54.15 The end of a title, or after a centered subhead in a manuscript:
Title: The Fall of Rome
Centered subhead: The First Cause

Hint 55. Use three spaced periods to indicate an omission.

55.1 These are called ellipsis periods and are useful when only part of a sentence or a verse of poetry is quoted:
". . . so shines a good deed in a naughty world."
55.2 When these three periods follow a complete sentence, a fourth period is added as a terminal period:
". . . that among these are life, liberty, and the pursuit of happiness . . . ."

Hint 56. Use a period properly with decimals, dollars, and cents.

56.1 Before a decimal: 6.25%; 0.17; 42,315.062.
56.2 Preceding cents written alone: $0.62; $0.19; $0.99.
56.3 Separating dollars and cents: $17.24; $26.11; $840.31.

Hint 57. Do not use two periods at the end of a quotation.
Wrong: He replied, "You may count on me.".
Right: He replied, "You may count on me."
Wrong: She said, "Every morning I sleep late.".
Right: She said, "Every morning I sleep late."
The same principle applies if the quotation ends with a question mark or an exclamation point:
Wrong: He asked, "What shall I do?".
Right: He asked, "What shall I do?"
Wrong: He exclaimed, "Great is thy glory, O King!".
Right: He exclaimed, "Great is thy glory, O King!"

NOW WORK THE EXERCISE ON PAGE 83

Exercise 35

	Right answers for page 81	Your answers for page 83

Trial I Place R if right: W, if wrong:

1. His speech had three parts: 1. the causes; 2. the costs; 3. the results. R ( )
2. He said, "I will come.". R ( )
3. It came C.O.D. R ( )
4. The concert is being presented at 2:00 p.m. and 8:00 p.m. R ( )
5. This serves ... as the cause of evil .... W ( )
6. Mr. and Mrs. R.D. Jones came to visit us. W ( )
7. He attended a meeting of the U.N. R ( )
8. It cost him $6,25. W ( )
9. The profit was 3.5% R ( )
10. "... of all sad words of tongue or pen, the saddest are ...." W ( )
11. I visited the gym. early in the morning. W ( )
12. He is a member of the AFL. R ( )
13. It was marked $0.62 cents. R ( )
14. John Jones, D.D. (b. 1920; d. 1954). W ( )
15. He said, "... of the people, by the people ...." R ( )

CHECK your answers with the right ones on page 85. If you have missed none, go ahead. If you missed one or more, try

Number wrong

Trial II Place R if Right; W, if wrong:

1. He answered, "I hate to get up in the morning!". W ( )
2. The orator said, "First in war, first in peace, and ...." W ( )
3. I have lab. today. R ( )
4. It cost him 0.69 cents. R ( )
5. He does not like the C.I.O. W ( )
6. It cost $6,325.46. W ( )
7. They called him Al. for short. R ( )
8. He received my memo yesterday. R ( )
9. Mr. and Mrs. William Young called today. W ( )
10. He asked me, "Is six o'clock too early". R ( )
11. "... if eyes are made for seeing, then beauty ...." W ( )
12. The price is .32 cents. R ( )
13. I heard it on CBS television. R ( )
14. France should cooperate in N.A.T.O. W ( )
15. Pat is one of my good friends. R ( )

AFTER MASTERY, TURN TO PAGE 84

Number wrong

Hints: End Punctuation — The Exclamation Point and the Question Mark

58.0 The exclamation point and the question mark are terminal marks in addition to the period. The period is used after declarative and weak imperative sentences. The exclamation point is used after strong exclamatory and imperative sentences. The question mark is used after a direct question.

Hint 58. Use the exclamation point after an expression of strong feeling.
If the statement is mild, do not use the exclamation point. End mildly exclamatory sentences with a period. The modern tendency is to avoid overuse of the exclamation point:
>   Help! Help! Come quickly!
>   Alas, I do not know what to do!
>   Mild emotion: I regret that he was unkind to me.
>   Mild emotion: Do not fail to register.

Hint 59. Use a question mark at the end of every direct question.

59.1 An indirect question repeats the thought but not the exact words of the speaker. It should be followed by the period, and not by the question mark.
>   Indirect question: He wanted to know what I should do.
>   Direct question: He asked, "What should you do?"
>   When did he call?
>   Are you coming to visit me?

59.2 Use question marks to indicate a series of queries in the same sentence:
>   Who will answer? You? Your brother? Your sister?
>   When did it happen? in 1920? 1930? or 1940?

59.3 Sometimes a question mark, enclosed in parentheses, is used to express doubt, uncertainty, or irony:
>   The ornament is a diamond (?) set in gold.
>   He is a pleasant (?) fellow. (Again, this usage should not be overworked)

59.4 In a polite request phrased as a question, good writers tend to use the period rather than the question mark. This is an example of rhetorical usage rather than grammatical.
>   Examples: May I expect to hear from you soon.
>   May I ask you to call on me after the game.

NOW WORK EXERCISE 36 ON PAGE 85.

Exercise 36

		Right answers for page 83	Your answers for page 85

Trial I   Place R if right; W, if wrong:

1. He asked me if I could work the problem? — R ( )
2. He made a heavy (?) attempt to smile. — W ( )
3. When will you make the trip? Next summer? Next winter? — W ( )
4. He asked me, "Are you ready?". — R ( )
5. I wouldn't have believed it of him! — R ( )
6. Oh, this might be much worse. — R ( )
7. Dear! Dear! I am frightened to death! — W ( )
8. May I hope to receive an answer soon. — W ( )
9. There's many a slip 'twixt the cup and the lip! — R ( )
10. Which is the best answer? Home? Street? Barn? — R ( )
11. The coat is of genuine (!) leather. — W ( )
12. He asked me whether or not I planned to buy a new car? — R ( )
13. Oh, this is unbearable! — W ( )
14. Did he say that you were a liar? — R ( )
15. Do you think you will return the favor? — R ( )

CHECK your answers with the right ones on page 87. If you missed none, go ahead. If you missed one or more, try

_____
Number wrong

Trial II   Place R if right; W, if wrong:

1. He asked me if I would return the book? — W ( )
2. Help! Murder! He's killing me! — R ( )
3. Who called me? Jack? Jim? Henry? — W ( )
4. He gave me an expensive (?) gift. — W ( )
5. Oh, don't ask that of me. — W ( )
6. Hip! Hip! Hurrah! We won! — R ( )
7. He asked you how to do it? — W ( )
8. Oh, please don't? — R ( )
9. Get out of here! You are a lousy thief! — R ( )
10. He exclaimed, "I knew it all the time!". — W ( )
11. May I hear from you soon. — R ( )
12. Then what did he say? — W ( )
13. It's never too late to mend. — R ( )
14. She asked him if he could come for dinner? — W ( )
15. Please! Please! I must have your attention! — R ( )

NOW TURN TO PAGE 86

_____
Number wrong

[85]

Hints: The Colon — Punctuation

60.0 The colon is usually a mark of introduction, and is more formal than the dash or the comma. In some respects you can think of it as an equality sign—that which precedes is the general statement; that which follows is the particulars.

Hint 60. Use the colon to introduce.

60.11 Introducing a list: He ordered the following articles: a saw, an axe, a plane, and a hammer.
60.12 Introducing a long report or quotation of one or more paragraphs.
60.13 Introducing a formal question: The question is: Will the people vote for this issue?
60.14 Introducing a second statement which explains the first: We know why he did it: he needed money.
60.15 Introducing a business letter: Dear Sir:; Gentlemen:.
60.16 Introducing a formal resolution: Resolved: That the United States accept the offer ....
60.17 Introducing a word, phrase, or clause where emphasis is desired: His aim in life is simple: girls. This is what he wants: her money.

60.2 Do not use the colon to separate prepositions from their objects or verbs from objects or complements.
   Wrong: I am fond of: music, sports, and plays.
   Right: I am fond of music, sports, and plays.
   Wrong: He bought: shoes and a hat.
   Right: He bought shoes and a hat.
   Wrong: His main concern is: wine, women, and song.
   Right: His main concern is wine, women, and song.
   Wrong: Some of our presidents, such as: Lincoln, Roosevelt, Truman, were deeply interested in the common people.
   Right: Some of our presidents, such as Lincoln, Roosevelt, Truman, were deeply interested in the common people. (*Such as* is preceded by a comma, but is never followed by a colon or a comma.)

60.3 Some unusual uses of the colon may be considered as separation rather than introduction:
60.31 Time: It is 8:35 a.m.
60.32 References: Matthew 22: 5-16.
60.33 Publishers: New York: American Book Company.
60.34 Titles: *Semantics: A College Textbook.*
60.35 Plays: Hamlet IV: 3.
60.36 Bible (Old Testament): The Lord is my shepherd: I shall not want.

(The modern tendency is away from the use of the colon as a mark of separation.)

NOW WORK EXERCISE ON PAGE 87.

Exercise 37

	Right answers for page 85	Your answers for page 87

Trial I   Place R if right; W, if wrong:

1. There are many kinds such as: flat, tall, round, and square. — W ( )
2. He began his business letter thus: Dear Sir: — R ( )
3. He named these three objects; paint, nails, and roofing. — R ( )
4. It occurred at 10:25 a.m. — W ( )
5. This is my intended purpose: a higher salary. — R ( )
6. Salutation of a friendly letter: Dear John, — R ( )
7. His reference was John 3;16. — R ( )
8. These are the three objects: a book, a pencil, a notebook. — R ( )
9. The problem is: What shall we do? — R ( )
10. He went to: Paris, Berlin, and Rome. — R ( )
11. The speaker spoke as follows: "We dread war; it is ...." — W ( )
12. This is the only right way: hard work. — W ( )
13. Thrift is good: honor is better. — R ( )
14. The four directions are: east, west, south, and north. — R ( )
15. The book is *Principles of English: A College Textbook*. — R ( )

CHECK your answers with the right ones on page 89. If you miss none, go ahead. If you miss one or more, try

Number wrong ____

Trial II   Place R if right; W, if wrong:

1. The reference is Luke 7:10-14. — W ( )
2. I like fruit such as: oranges, pears, and apples. — R ( )
3. This is exactly what I need: your real help. — R ( )
4. He ordered the following; paper, pencils, and pens. — R ( )
5. It occurred at 6;30 a.m. in the morning. — R ( )
6. He then spoke as follows: (six paragraphs) — R ( )
7. He began his business letter thus: Gentlemen: — W ( )
8. I am fond of: wrestling, boxing, and skating. — W ( )
9. My text is *Principles of Geology: A College Textbook*. — R ( )
10. All may be summed up in one word: perseverance. — W ( )
11. He invested in: real estate and bonds. — R ( )
12. I hate: hardwork, late hours, low pay. — R ( )
13. He appointed the following: Jim Jones, Kit Carson, and me. — R ( )
14. I know only one thing: I wanted that promotion. — W ( )
15. The ingredients are: flour, milk, sugar, and yeast. — R ( )

AFTER MASTERY, TURN TO PAGE 88

Number wrong ____

[87]

Hints: The Dash—The Versatile Mark

61.0 The dash is the most dramatic and versatile of the marks of punctuation. It loses these qualities if overworked. It may serve the purpose of introduction, termination, separation, or enclosure. Do not use it as a careless substitute for the comma, colon, or period, although it is true that often the dash is a proper substitute for these marks. Here apply your rhetorical rather than your grammatical sense.

Hint 61. Use the dash to show a sudden abrupt break, shift, or turn in thought or structure.
>   I thought—but do you care to hear?
>   Should we—dare we—do this thing?

61.1 The dash may be used to indicate an interruption, an unfinished statement, or an unfinished word:
>   "I don't know what to answer—" and then he turned away.
>   Now—will you believe me?—I know what you mean.

61.2 The dash may be used to introduce a word, phrase, or clause when emphasis is desired:
>   He gave me my award—a ten-dollar bill.

61.3 The dash may be used to set off a parenthetical statement (For this purpose the comma is weaker and the parenthesis stronger than the dash):
>   My father—he is a teacher—taught me this.
>   My suggestion—please pardon me—is that you leave at once.

61.4 The dash may be used to indicate omission of letters or words, or to connect combinations of letters or words:
>   Mr. A—answered immediately.
>   Closed Saturday; open Monday—Friday.

61.5 The dash may be used to precede an author's name after a direct quotation:
>   No army can withstand the strength of an idea whose time has come.
>   —Victor Hugo
>   The man who is prepared has the battle half fought.
>   —Cervantes

Hint 62. Use the dash to introduce a summarizing clause.
Usually it separates a summarizing clause beginning with *such, these, all, those* from a series preceding it:
>   Excitement, dates, parties, sports, hard study—all of these are part of your freshman year.
>   Honor, integrity, valor—these are the marks of a gentleman.

NOW WORK THE EXERCISE ON PAGE 89

Exercise 38

		Right answers for page 87	Your answers for page 89
Trial I	Place R if right; W, if wrong:		
1.	You have seen my wife—gentle, dainty, and gracious.	W	( )
2.	English, math, Latin, these caused me to fail.	R	( )
3.	His plans appeared possible, to travel by air.	W	( )
4.	He is an engineer on the Columbus—Toledo run.	R	( )
5.	None—but the brave—deserve the fair.	R	( )
6.	One need she has greater than any other—attention.	R	( )
7.	We will go; we promise you; without delay.	W	( )
8.	Let me answer you—but will it do any good?	R	( )
9.	Please write out exercises 14–17 for tomorrow.	R	( )
10.	John said, "You know I—" "Shut up!" she snapped.	W	( )
11.	A home, a job, a wife—what more do I want?	R	( )
12.	Our next job is; to build a garage.	R	( )
13.	I'll give—let's see—a dollar for that cause.	W	( )
14.	If I hesitate—I surely will not; what then?	W	( )
15.	Chairman W— answered the question.	R	( )

CHECK your answers with the right ones on page 91. If you miss none, go ahead. If you miss one or more, then try

Number wrong

Trial II	Place R if right; W, if wrong:		
1.	Wine, women, and song, these were his downfall.	R	( )
2.	His intentions were noble, to give her help.	W	( )
3.	You know my son—grinning, awkward, always hungry.	R	( )
4.	Captain H— gave that order.	W	( )
5.	Our next order is; to build a boat.	W	( )
6.	Tell me—now that you know—would you do it?	R	( )
7.	Ahem! No; yes; maybe! will you?	R	( )
8.	Purity, beauty, modesty, these characterize our queen.	W	( )
9.	I shall try—but do you expect results?	R	( )
10.	Unknown to him are; honesty, hope, hard work.	R	( )
11.	This was his award—a five dollar bill.	W	( )
12.	For tomorrow study pages 21–45.	W	( )
13.	Mr. A— told Mr. B—, "You are a liar!"	R	( )
14.	We hope to; yes, you are right; go next day.	R	( )
15.	In the sentence, *I saw a pretty girl*, use a period, not a dash after *the pretty girl*.	W	( )

AFTER MASTERY, TURN TO PAGE 90

Number wrong

Hints: The Comma-Separating Punctuation

63.0 The comma has many distinct and varied uses. *Close* punctuation (using many commas or other marks) tends to be the usual practice in formal writing, but in informal writing, such as description, narration, journalistic, and business writing, *open* punctuation (using a few commas or other marks) tends to prevail. The tendency is toward *open* punctuation. An error may arise when the comma is used as a mark of separation instead of the semicolon or the period. This error, known as the comma splice, has been treated earlier in this workbook.

Hint 63. Use a comma after a long introductory phrase or dependent clause.
(Let's leave it up to you to decide rhetorically whether the introductory statement is long or short.)
    Short phrase: Right: On Tuesday he came home.
    Long phrase: Right: By working long hours after school, John earned money to go to college.
    Long clause: Right: When the moon comes over the mountain, I'll be waiting for you.

Hint 64. Use a comma to separate long independent clauses joined by the usual coordinating conjunctions.

64.1 These common coordinating conjunctions are *and, but, nor, or,* and *for. For* is particularly dangerous, as the omission of the comma may cause a misreading:
    Wrong: I came yesterday morning for my girl asked me to see her.
    Right: I came yesterday morning, for my girl asked me to see her.
    Right: I came early in the week, but I did not stay.
    Right: He will not answer his phone, nor will he leave his room.

64.2 If these clauses are short, the comma is often omitted:
    Right: I called but no one answered.

Hint 65. Use a comma to prevent misreading.
    Wrong: Inside the cat was sleeping peacefully.
    Wrong: Outside the garage needs painting.
    Wrong: He called for my parents were home.
    Corrections: Inside, the cat .... Outside, the garage, ... He called, for ....

Hint 66. Use commas to separate words, phrases, or clauses in a series.
The problem is: Shall we say a, b and c; or a, b, and c? Some languages other than English and some workers in English omit the comma before *and*. We advocate the use of the comma (and the best style books do the same), for clarity's sake:
    Confusing: She ate honey, bread and milk (two foods or three?).
    Clear: She ate honey, bread, and milk.
    Right: Our flag is red, white, and blue.

Exercise 39

		Right answers for page 89	Your answers for page 91
Trial I	Place R if right; W, if wrong:		
1.	After eating my sister went to the show.	R	( )
2.	After a long and tiring introduction, he spoke on the issue.	W	( )
3.	On Wednesday he went to town.	W	( )
4.	The bell rang, she went to the door.	R	( )
5.	He studies in the morning, but I study in the afternoon.	W	( )
6.	To succeed in life, one must work hard.	R	( )
7.	I did not go for my father told me not to.	W	( )
8.	The three who went were Tom, Dick and Harry.	R	( )
9.	He closed the gate, knocked on the door and waited.	R	( )
10.	At five o'clock he went home.	R	( )
11.	He ate candy, cake, and fruit.	R	( )
12.	Whenever the weather threatens to storm, I stay home.	W	( )
13.	He called to me, I didn't hear him.	R	( )
14.	She agreed to go but, he didn't keep his word.	W	( )
15.	He ran for the sheriff was chasing him.	R	( )

CHECK your answers with the right ones on page 93. If you miss none, go ahead. If you miss one or more, try

Number wrong _____

Trial II	Place R if right; W, if wrong:		
1.	After a pleasant evening at the concert, I went to bed.	W	( )
2.	After shooting my teacher looked for the rabbit.	W	( )
3.	He ran for the skunk was in his road.	R	( )
4.	We ordered these materials: sand, cement, and plaster.	R	( )
5.	Jim, Jack, and John visited us yesterday.	W	( )
6.	The king marched up the hill, and then he marched down again.	R	( )
7.	On Thursday; he delivered the letter.	W	( )
8.	Inside the tiger growled to get out.	W	( )
9.	He ran for my aunt heard him.	R	( )
10.	Our flag is red and white and blue.	W	( )
11.	Our flag is red, white, and blue.	R	( )
12.	Our flag is red, white and blue.	R	( )
13.	He ate oatmeal, toast and coffee.	R	( )
14.	He will neither run for sheriff, nor will he turn us down.	W	( )

AFTER MASTERY, TURN TO PAGE 92   R

Number wrong _____

Hints: The Comma – Enclosing — Punctuation

67.0 We may use the comma, the dash, the parentheses to indicate enclosing: the comma indicates the least pause; the parentheses, the most formal and greatest; and the dash, informal in its effect, lies between the two.

> Commas: John Jones, living at home, won the prize.
> Dashes: We are opposed—and we mean seriously opposed—to this candidate.
> Parentheses: Early in the century (the date 1910 is important), this king came into power.

Hint 67. Use a comma to enclose nonrestrictive phrases and clauses.
To test whether or not a phrase or clause is nonrestrictive, try leaving it out of the sentence. If the meaning of the sentence is changed, the omitted phrase or clause is restrictive and necessary for the meaning. Restrictive clauses are not enclosed by commas.

> Nonrestrictive: This runner, breathing easily, won the race.
> Restrictive: The runner who was breathing easily won the race.
> Nonrestrictive: *Treasure Island,* which tells of pirates, is interesting.
> Restrictive: The book which describes pirates is interesting.

Hint 68. Use commas to enclose words, phrases, or clauses loosely inserted into the sentence.

68.1 The following are examples of various kinds:
- 68.11 Mild exclamation: She is, well, rather busy.
- 68.12 Yes and no: Yes, she is my sister.
- 68.13 The appositive: Harry Lyons, the senior, is my roommate.
- 68.14 Absolute phrases: The test completed, we went home.
- 68.15 Direct address: It is, Mr. Jones, a great success.
- 68.16 Omission of words understood: Mary writes fiction; John, poetry.
- 68.17 Dates: On Sunday, July 4, 1865, our hero was born.
- 68.18 Names and addresses: 758 Francis Ave., Columbus 9, Ohio
- 68.19 After the salutation in a friendly letter: Dear Jane,
- 68.19.1 After the complimentary close of all letters: Yours truly,

68.2 Miscellaneous uses of the comma:
- 68.21 Introductory phrases with a direct quotation: "Is he the one," I asked, "who hit you?"
- 68.22 Titles following a name: John Jones, A.B., M.D.
- 68.23 Numbers of four or more digits: There were 6,432 answers.

NOW WORK THE EXERCISE ON PAGE 93

Exercise 40

		Right answers for page 91	Your answers for page 93
Trial I	Place R if right; W, if wrong.		

1.	The house, that Jack built, has been sold.	W	( )
2.	I like toast and coffee, milk and honey.	R	( )
3.	I bought apples, pears, and peaches.	R	( )
4.	He who works at his task will gain favor.	W	( )
5.	In a business letter, place a comma after "Dear Sir,"	R	( )
6.	And now sir, what shall we do?	R	( )
7.	On June 11, 1962, he returned to England.	W	( )
8.	This was the goose, that laid the golden egg.	W	( )
9.	No I will not do it.	W	( )
10.	Jack Stout, my coach, helped me.	R	( )
11.	The ticket, which admits you, is cheaper.	R	( )
12.	Yours truly;	R	( )
13.	Jack plays baseball, Jim; football.	W	( )
14.	He is as you know, a poor loser.	W	( )
15.	Will you please, Sir, answer me?	W	( )

CHECK your answers with the right ones on Page 95. If you missed none, go ahead. If you missed one or more, try

Number wrong

Trial II   Place R if right; W, if wrong:

1.	The ship, wrecked on the shore, is the Hesperus.	R	( )
2.	No; she is my aunt.	W	( )
3.	Jack Kearns the junior, played the lead.	W	( )
4.	"Is she the one," I asked, "who called me?"	R	( )
5.	This is the correct conclusion to a business letter: Yours Truly;	R	( )
6.	It is Mr. Smith, a great honor.	R	( )
7.	Robert Smith; A.B.; M.D.	W	( )
8.	The lady you wished to meet is my aunt.	W	( )
9.	My mother, who spoke graciously of you, has invited you to dinner.	W	( )
10.	He lives in Somerset, Ohio.	R	( )
11.	He bought 11,465 boxes of fruit in the past year.	R	( )
12.	Having bathed the lady returned to her hotel.	W	( )
13.	I bought bread, butter, milk, and cream.	W	( )
14.	He is as you know a very rich man.	R	( )
15.	Please, dear Sir, give me a dime.		( )

AFTER MASTERY, TURN TO PAGE 94

Number wrong

Review   Punctuation

Let's pause in our progress and take a test!

Review all errors and difficulties since the last test.

Grade yourself on your first attempt, using our scale. You will recall it looks like this:

ERRORS	GRADE
0 - 2	A
3 - 4	B
5 - 6	C
7 - 8	D
More than 8	F, or failed

If you make an A or even a B, you are making good progress. If your grade is C or lower, give yourself a thorough review till you can be sure of mastery.

Note the right answers in the Key on page 97 and references to the Hints for each item missed.

NOW TRY WITH COURAGE!
(I am wishing you "Smooth Sailing")

Review Test VI

	Right answers for page 93	Your answers for page 95
Review Test VI Place R if right; W, if wrong:		
1. General U.S. Grant, one of our presidents, fought in the Civil War.	W	( )
2. Please buy: sugar, bread and butter.	R	( )
3. She smiled at me, I scowled back.	R	( )
4. I hoped—is this important to you?	R	( )
5. Faith, hope, and charity—these are important traits.	W	( )
6. He knocked but no one came.	W	( )
7. My wish—I hate to say this—is that you leave at once!	R	( )
8. That tall man who just waved to me is my father.	W	( )
9. He went for the cow had run away.	W	( )
10. After scrubbing the maid cooked our meals.	R	( )
11. This is the correct salutation of a business letter: Dear Sir;	W	( )
12. This is the correct complimentary close for a business letter: Yours truly,	W	( )
	W	( )
13. This is Mr. Hill, a great honor.	W	( )
14. May I offer the following resolution: (five paragraphs)	R	( )
15. The text is Luke VIII;3.		( )
16. After a long and weary struggle, he gave up.		( )
17. Walter Short the policeman caught the thief.		( )
18. "This is the boy," I said, "who did the good deed."		( )
19. Would you—like—maybe—to buy something?		( )
20. He is full of: vim, vigor, and vitality.		( )
21. The population of this city is 32,714.	W	( )
22. After shooting the hunter loaded his gun.	W	( )
23. It occurred early in the morning, but we did not know about it till the next day.	W	
	R	( )
24. She smiled—I couldn't refuse her—and I bought six tickets.	W	( )
25. She said, "Please call.".	W	( )
26. Please, Miss White, attend our party.	W	( )
27. He went for the bear was angry.	R	( )
28. He looked at her fondly, she looked far away.	R	( )
29. Our needs are: men, money, and support.	R	( )
30. Smile—don't interrupt me—smile, I say!	R	( )
	W	
AFTER MASTERY, TURN TO PAGE 96	R	
	W	Number wrong
	R	
		Grade ___

[95]

Hints: The Semicolon   Punctuation

69.0   The semicolon should be used only as a mark of separation. Think of it as a strong comma or a weak period. It should not be substituted for the dash as a summarizing mark or for the colon as an introductory mark:
> Wrong: Math, English, Latin; these give me the most trouble.
> Right: Math, English, Latin—these give me the most trouble.
> Wrong: Dear Sir;   Right: Dear Sir:

Hint 69. Use the semicolon as a cure for the comma splice.
> Wrong: He came to town, she soon followed him.
> Right: He came to town; she soon followed him.
> Wrong: The door opened, he came into the room.
> Right: The door opened; he came into the room.

Hint 70. Use the semicolon between two independent clauses not connected by a coordinating conjunction. (If you use a comma, you have a comma splice!)

70.1   It will be recalled that the coordinating conjunctions are *and, but, or, nor,* and *for.* When one of these is used, it is preceded by the comma:
> Right: The day was long and dreary, but the evening was pleasant.
> Right: The day was long and dreary; the evening was pleasant.

70.2   If the clauses are long or contain internal punctuation, use the semicolon, even if these clauses are joined by a conjunction:
> Right: His course was long, difficult, and expensive; but John made effort after effort, trial after trial.

Hint 71. Use the semicolon between coordinate clauses when conjunctive adverbs are used.
Some conjunctive adverbs are *therefore, however, hence, accordingly, furthermore, nevertheless, consequently, thus, then, yet, for instance, for example,* etc.:
> Right: College is difficult; *therefore* you must study.
> Right: Jim is lazy; he is, *in fact,* the laziest man I know.
> Right: I speak German; my children, *however,* can not speak it.
> Right: He arose early; *nevertheless,* he accomplished very little.
> Right: Our lane is very rough; *hence,* cars approach our house slowly.

(Rhetorically you may or may not use a comma after a conjunctive adverb)

Hint 72. Use the semicolon to group items in a series.
> Right: The members of the committee are Mr. Jones, chairman; Miss Smith, secretary; and Miss Black, treasurer.

NOW WORK THE EXERCISE ON PAGE 97

Exercise 41

	Right answers for page 95	Your answers for page 97
Trial I Place R if right; W, if wrong:		

1. He began his business letter: Dear Sir;   R–67   ( )
2. He bought the following; a saw, a hammer, and nails.   W–66 & 60.2   ( )
3. His work was done; therefore, he returned home.   W–63   ( )
4. Jim, an athlete, loved sports; Mary, a musician, loved opera.   R–61.1   ( )
5. I love baseball, I hate to attend lectures.   R–62   ( )
6. She knocked at my door; I opened it and greeted her.   R–64.2   ( )
7. He ordered the following; a hamburger, a glass of juice, and coffee.   R–61.3   ( )
8. He signed the letter: Yours truly;   R–67   ( )
9. Quarrelling, fighting, insulting one another; these I hate.   W–64.1   ( )
10. She never answered me, I never wrote her again.   W–65   ( )
11. The officers are as follows: Jim Henry, chairman; Bill Smith, secretary; and Ann Brown, treasurer.   W–60.15   ( )
12. Our colors are these: green, white, and purple.   R–68.19.1   ( )
13. These are the important dates; December 25 and July 4.   W–68.15   ( )
14. She often hesitated; for instance, at the party last night.   R–60.12   ( )
15. He was tired, therefore he went to bed.   W–60.32   ( )

CHECK your answers with the right ones on Page 99. If you missed none, go ahead. If you missed one or more, try

Number wrong

	Right answers	
	R–63	
	W–68.13	
	R–68.21	
	R–61.1	
	W–60.2	
	R–68.23	
	W–65	

Trial II   Place R if right; W, if wrong:

1. Jim, a freshman, lives at home; Jack a junior, lives in a fraternity house.   ( )
2. I went to the game; I enjoyed it very much.   R–64   ( )
3. Friends; listen to my advice.   R–61.1   ( )
4. He gave me the following; a book, a pencil, and a knife.   W–57   ( )
5. He worked on the farm, she got a job in the city.   R–68.15   ( )
6. She was not a cautious woman; for instance, she never locked the doors of her home.   W–64.1   ( )
7. He came to town; but, nevertheless, he didn't join us.   W–63   ( )
8. He met me on the street; he did not speak.   W–60.2   ( )
9. He went to the bag; twice he fanned; then he knocked a home run.   R–61.1   ( )
10. Please order these; pop, ice cream, and wieners.   ( )
11. Men, women, children; all attended the parade.   ( )
12. Inflation hurts me seriously, I don't get much for my money.   ( )
13. Sometimes we wonder; what are his intentions?   ( )
14. Study hard; ask questions; do your best.   ( )
15. Jim, a freshman, always hands his work in promptly; Joe, his brother, and a senior, never does his work on time.   ( )

AFTER MASTERY, TURN TO PAGE 98

Number wrong

Hints: Parentheses / Brackets Punctuation

73.0   Parentheses and brackets are marks of enclosure. Commas may be used to enclose material closely related to the thought of the sentence; dashes may be used to enclose informal material a little more remote in meaning; and parentheses may be used to set off the most distant material, particularly if a formal effect is desired. Brackets are editorial parentheses and enclose editorial remarks that are inserted for explanation in someone else's copy. Brackets are used so infrequently that this symbol does not appear on the ordinary typewriter.

Hint 73. Use parentheses to set off remote material.

73.1   Here are some common uses of parentheses:
    73.11   To enclose letters or figures in an enumeration:
        She sent him money (1) to pay his tuition; (2) to buy books.
    73.12   To enclose helps or directions:
        This rule (see page 42) will help you.
    73.13   To enclose a question mark indicating uncertainty with respect to the previous statement:
        Born in 1950 (?), he has lived in Ohio all his life.
        His frankness (?) alarmed me.
    73.14   To repeat or verify business figures:
        The price is $2,000.00 (two thousand dollars).
    73.15   To enclose remote material inserted into the sentence:
        Right: This book (I recommend it highly) should be in your library.
        Right: His approach (do you agree with me?) is pleasing.
        Right: His answer (he ought to know better) was insulting.

73.2   Other marks of punctuation follow the second parenthesis unless the mark belongs to the parenthetical material:
        I believe her (and I know why I did).
        He praised us (and it was sheer flattery!); for he had his reasons.
        He asked her (did you ever see the like?), and she accepted.
(The parenthetical material may or may not begin with a capital.)

Hint 74. Use brackets to enclose editorial comment.

This may be mere comment, correction, or interpolation in a quoted passage:
74.1   To mark errors: I seen [sic] him.
74.2   To enclose editorial data: In the summer [1776] the document was signed.
74.3   To enclose stage directions: Elinor [stepping to the center of the stage] : Let's get to the point!

NOW WORK EXERCISE ON PAGE 99

Exercise 42

	Right answers for page 97	Your answers for page 99

Trial I Place R if right; W, if wrong:

1. Tom Jones, the quarterback, will be elected captain. — W ( )
2. Tom Jones—this was a surprise to all—was elected captain. — W ( )
3. Dick Wright (please note our prediction here) will be elected president of the senior class. — R ( )
4. Bob Edmunds [his full name is Robert Henry Edmunds] was chosen to be secretary of the bowling league. — W / R ( )
5. I ought to have knowed [sic] better. — W ( )
6. He offered (1) to pay the bill; (2) to provide the car; and, thirdly, to meet him at the station. — W / W ( )
7. He was born in Columbus (?) in 1810. — W ( )
8. The reference (see Sec. V) is correct. — ( )
9. I am sending you $50 (fifty dollars). — R ( )
10. Jim [assuming an attitude of grief]: "Woe is me!" — R ( )
11. Mary my beautiful sister never helps with the cooking. — W ( )
12. The price—and you can trust us—is right. — R ( )
13. He signed the letter: Respectively [sic] yours. — W ( )
14. This battle, fought in 1943 (?), won the war. — ( )
15. If you will join me (I ask you seriously to consider this), write me. — ( )

CHECK your answers with the right ones on page 101. If you missed none, go ahead. If you missed one or more, try

Number wrong _____

Trial II Place R if right; W, if wrong:

R
R

1. If ever you need money (I hope you never will), call on me. — W ( )
2. Please seperete [sic] it from the rest. — W ( )
3. John (my brother), answered him. — W ( )
4. Rick (his real name is Richard) answered me. — ( )
5. This story—see Chapter V—is remarkable. — R ( )
6. John, John, the piper's son, stole a pig. — R ( )
7. I received your check for seventy dollars [$70]. — R ( )
8. He said he wrote it at the age of sixteen [Critics doubt that he did]. — R ( )
9. Here are three reasons: (1) He often lies; (2) He never works; (3) He never pays. — W / W ( )
10. In that year [1863], the document was signed. — W ( )
11. My daughter, pretty as a picture, won all hearts. — W ( )
12. The chart (see page 80) will help you. — R ( )
13. On the other hand—I say this gently—the matter is none of your business. — ( )
14. You will find eighty dollars ($80.00) enclosed. — R ( )
15. And now, if you please, let us proceed. — ( )

AFTER MASTERY, TURN TO PAGE 100

Number wrong _____

[99]

Hints: The Hyphen Punctuation

75.0 The hyphen is a mark of separation used only between parts of a word. It is not the *dash*. Here is how the hyphen is gained and lost as our language develops: first, when two words are associated, they are written separately—*class room;* secondly, as they grow to be more of a unit in common usage, they are hyphenated (that is, a hyphen is used between them)—class-room; finally, they are written as one word—*classroom.* Rules are not adequate to regulate this change, and your dictionary is the best authority when you are in doubt. The modern dictionary now uses an elevated dot between syllables, reserving the hyphen for compound words: syl·lab·i·ca·tion; re-echo.

Hint 75. Use a hyphen to separate the parts of many compound words.
Examples: son-in-law; go-between; ex-president; self-indictment.

75.1 A compound adjective before a noun is hyphenated; if it follows, it is not:
A *well-dressed* gentleman entered the room.
The gentleman was well dressed.

75.2 Compound numbers from twenty-one to ninety-nine and fractions are hyphenated:
There are *twenty-two* sophomores in my class.
He played *two-thirds* of the game.

75.3 Often the hyphen is used to avoid ambiguity:
He owns a *co-op.* He really needs *re-creation.*

75.4 The hyphen may be used to designate stuttering or the spelling out of words:
"Ma-a-a-ay-I-I-I-see-see you h-home?"
"Does b-e-a-r spell lion or tiger?"

Hint 76. Avoid careless syllabication.

76.1 If a long word must be divided, place the hyphen at the end of the first line and not at the beginning of the second:
His *ask-*
ing me caused all this excitement.

76.2 Never divide a word of one syllable:
Wrong: *a-che; fr-iend*

76.3 Avoid a one-letter syllable in the division:
Wrong: *a-meliorate; phenomen-a.*

76.4 Avoid dividing proper names: Thomas *Jeffer-*
son.

76.5 Avoid separating the name and the initials that go with it: *T.S.*
Eliot

76.6 Avoid two or more hyphens per word: *self-improve-ment; non-sen-si-cal.*

NOW WORK THE EXERCISE ON PAGE 101

Exercise 43

	Right answers for page 99	Your answers for page 101
Trial I Place R if right; W, if wrong:		
1. I love my motherinlaw.	R	( )
2. A fast moving freight hit the automobile.	R	( )
3. Many long-playing records are delightful entertainment.	R	( )
4. Thirty-six members form this team.	R	( )
5. Spell it this way: b-e-l-i-e-v-e.	R	( )
6. This so-called medicine is four-fifths alcohol.	R	( )
7. "T-t-tell me your name," he stuttered.	R	( )
8. He works a forty-hour week.	R	( )
9. These words may be divided thus: syll-able; o-ral; e-xit.	W	( )
10. Proper recreation is really re-creation.	R	( )
11. Our ex-president is a courageous man.	R	( )
12. This ex-ample is not a good one.	W	( )
13. He is a regular know-it-all.	W	( )
14. He is the quarter-back on our team.	W	( )
15. It took him many hours to come to the realization of his problem.	R	( )

CHECK your answers with the right ones on page 103. If you missed none, go ahead. If you missed one or more, try

Number wrong

Trial II Place R if right; W, if wrong:		
1. My father-in-law gave me this watch.	R	( )
2. A rough-looking fellow accosted me.	R	( )
3. The bill was finally passed by a three fourths majority.	W	( )
4. The pre-enrollment was heavy.	R	( )
5. Spell it this way: r-e-c-e-i-v-e.	W	( )
6. Our expresident appeared before us.	W	( )
7. He is the half-back on our team.	R	( )
8. An ever-rising tide of opposition was evident.	W	( )
9. An uneven right-hand margin may be necessary.	R	( )
10. This e-vent occurred last year.	W	( )
11. He paid fifty-five dollars for the suit.	R	( )
12. The man was well known for oratory.	R	( )
13. This well known man visited me.	W	( )
14. "H-h-h-how do-o-o you do-o!" he stuttered.	R	( )
15. This son-in-law of mine is a Jack-of-all-trades.	R	( )

AFTER MASTERY, TURN TO PAGE 102

Number wrong

Hints: The Apostrophe — Punctuation

77.0 The apostrophe has three general uses: to show the possessive case; to show the omission of letters or figures; and to show the plural of figures, letters, and symbols.

Hint 77. Use the apostrophe and *s* to indicate the possessive case.

77.1 Nouns not ending in *s:*
>   This store sells men's, women's, and children's clothing.
>   Our team's new uniforms are purple and white.

77.2 Plural nouns ending in *s:* Use the apostrophe alone:
>   The boys' team won. He took a two-weeks' vacation trip.

77.3 Singular nouns ending in *s* or the *s* sound may add only the apostrophe to avoid difficult or unpleasant pronunciation:
>   Keats' poems; Robert Burns's life or Robert Burns' life; for conscience' sake; Demosthenes' orations.

77.4 Joint possession. Add *'s* to the last word: Mary and Jane's room is always neat (one room). Smith and White's grocery sells these cereals (one store).

77.5 Individual possession. Add *'s* to each word: Jack's and Jim's boats are for sale (two boats). He cleaned Bill's and John's suits (two suits).

77.6 Hyphenated or compound words. Add *'s* only to the last word: This was his father-in-law's business.

77.7 Indefinite pronouns. Add *'s:* anybody's; someone's.

Hint 78. Do not use the apostrophe with personal or relative pronouns.
>   Wrong: our's, his', it's, their's, who's.
>   Right: ours, his, its, theirs, whose.

Remember *it's* is always short for *it is,* and is not the possessive of *it.*

Hint 79. Use the apostrophe to show that letters or figures have been omitted.
>   Examples: Class of '10; o'clock; it's; don't; doesn't; isn't; he's.
>   John's hat isn't here. It's a long time till ten o'clock.

Hint 80. Use the apostrophe to show the plurals of letters, numbers, symbols, and words when used as symbols.
>   Symbol words: Don't overwork *for's* and *so's* in writing.
>   Letters: I always forget to dot my *i*'s.
>   Numbers: My *3*'s look like *s*'s.
>   Symbols: Rights are +'s and wrongs are -'s.

80.1 The apostrophe should not be used to form the plural of proper nouns:
>   Wrong: The Young's came to dinner.
>   Right: The Youngs came to dinner.

NOW WORK THE EXERCISE ON PAGE 103.

Exercise 44

		Right answers for page 101	Your answers for page 103
Trial I	Place R if right; W, if wrong:		
1.	Do'nt reply to his letter.	W	( )
2.	I visited the White's.	W	( )
3.	It's worth exceeds five hundred dollars.	R	( )
4.	Whose car is that?	R	( )
5.	I took a three-week's vacation.	R	( )
6.	It was his mother's-in-law address.	R	( )
7.	Mind your ps and qs.	R	( )
8.	Aristophanes's plays are modern in thought.	R	( )
9.	Moses's reply was quiet.	W	( )
10.	He did his best.	R	( )
11.	He bought John and Jim's share (one share).	R	( )
12.	She took care of Mrs. Brown's and Mrs. White's children (two groups of children).	W R	( )
13.	It was as clean as a hound's tooth.	W	( )
14.	Your 8s are not clear.		( )
15.	This is the dentist's office.	R	( )

CHECK your answers with the right ones on Page 105. If you missed none, go ahead. If you missed one or more, try

Number wrong

Trial II	Place R if right; W, if wrong:		
1.	The Jones's came to visit us.	R	( )
2.	I always forget to cross my ts.	R	( )
3.	Homers address aint known to many.	W	( )
4.	It is 8 p.m. oclock.	R	( )
5.	For conscience' sake, do it.	R	( )
6.	Moses' tablets were of stone.	W	( )
7.	The mens' team defeated the womens'.	W	( )
8.	Jack's and Harold's golf clubs are different.	R	( )
9.	I bought it at Miller's and White's store.	R	( )
10.	This is my mother-in-law's automobile.	W	( )
11.	Dot your i-s and cross your t-s.	R	( )
12.	Don't give up the ship!	R	( )
13.	It's a long way to Tipperary.	W	( )
14.	The beautiful river wends it's weary way.	R	( )
15.	For goodness' sake, spare me that ordeal.	R	( )

AFTER MASTERY, TURN TO PAGE 104

Number wrong

Review   Punctuation

Time again for another test!

Review all errors and difficulties since the last test.

Grade yourself on your first attempt, using our scale. You will recall it looks like this:

ERRORS	GRADE
0 - 2	A
3 - 4	B
5 - 6	C
7 - 8	D
More than 8	F, or failed

If you make an A or even a B, you are making good progress. If your grade is C or lower, plan a thorough review with the hope of ultimate mastery.

Note the right answers in the Key on page 107 and references to the Hints for each item missed.

NOW TAKE THE TEST ON PAGE 105
(We all are rooting for you!)

Review Test VII

		Right answers for page 103	Your answers for page 105
Review Test VII	Place R if right; W, if wrong:		
1.	Its on it's way to it's destination.	W	( )
2.	The boys' chorus outnumbered the girls'.	W	( )
3.	Who's hat are you wearing?	W	( )
4.	My 3's look like my 8's.	R	( )
5.	He dont come round no more.	W	( )
6.	I have a well-worn volume of Keats' poems.	W	( )
7.	That book is her's.	W	( )
8.	The Clark's visited us last evening.	W	( )
9.	It's travels took many days.	W	( )
10.	Joe's and Mary's shop has good trade (one shop).	R	( )
11.	He did not enjoy his mother's-in-law visit.	R	( )
12.	Jim's coat isn't in the closet.		( )
13.	The price is $2,050 (two thousand and fifty dollars).	R	( )
14.	He done [sic] him wrong.	R	( )
15.	Please order these; steaks, bread, butter, and milk.	W	( )
16.	The morning was fair; the afternoon, rainy.	R	( )
17.	He was lazy, therefore he wouldn't work.		( )
18.	This is the correct salutation for a business letter: Dear Sir;		( )
19.	Spell it this way: l-e-i-s-u-r-e.		( )
20.	Wine, women, and song; these were his downfall.		( )
21.	He went to the farm; but, nevertheless, he didn't work.		( )
22.	The officers are Smith, chairman; Jones, secretary; and Brown, treasurer.	W	( )
23.	The work was long and difficult, but we finished it.	W	( )
24.	The road was very rough; hence, we arrived late.	W	( )
25.	He played two-thirds of the game.	W	( )
26.	He came to our home, he didn't stay long.	R	( )
27.	That year [1914] the great struggle began.	R	( )
28.	His courtesy (?) pleased the old lady.	W	( )
29.	A tough-looking tramp knocked at our door.	R	( )
30.	The co-op wouldn't sell it to him.	W	( )

AFTER MASTERY, TURN TO PAGE 106

R
W
R
R
W
R

Number wrong _____

Grade _____

Hints: Quotation Marks — Punctuation

81.0   Quotation is repetition of what someone said or wrote. Double quotation marks enclose complete direct quotation, and single quotation marks enclose a quotation within a quotation. Quotation marks always come in pairs. Do not omit either one of the pairs. No quotation marks are used with an indirect quotation.

Hint 81. Use double quotation marks to enclose direct quotation.

81.1   A complete quotation: Jim said, "I shall return tomorrow."
81.2   An interrupted quotation: "I shall return," said Jim, "tomorrow at noon."
81.3   In dialogue: "Who is to come?" John asked.
                     "Everybody," Mary answered.
81.4   Lengthy quotation. In lengthy quotations involving several paragraphs, place quotation marks at the beginning of each paragraph but at the end of *only* the last paragraph. However, most writers prefer to indent the quoted material and use single-space rather than quotation marks.
81.5   Titles of stories, poems, songs, chapters, articles, and other subdivisions of a printed publication:
            Story: He read Irving's "Rip Van Winkle."
            Poem: He preferred Bryant's "Thanatopsis."
            Chapter: One chapter of the book, *College Teaching*, is called "How to Measure."
       (Summarizing quotation marks and italics: use italics for books; use quotation marks for chapters.)
81.6   Words used as definition, slang, or nickname:
            Definition: Distinguish "clever" from "intelligent."
            Slang: This assertion is pure "tommy-rot."
            Nickname: "Toughie" White lives up to his name.

Hint 82. Use single quotation marks to enclose a quotation within a quotation.
            Example: He replied, "I know he asked, 'What shall I do?' "
82.1   To punctuate a quotation within a quotation within a quotation, the order is double marks, single marks, double marks. This awkward construction should be used rarely.
            Example: I heard him say, "It was Jim who said to me, 'I love the quotation, "Give me liberty or give me death!" ' "

Hint 83. Place quotation marks correctly with respect to other marks.

83.1   The comma and the period are always placed within the quotation marks (See previous examples).
83.2   The colon and the semicolon are placed outside the quotation marks: I read "The Legend of Sleepy Hollow"; I enjoyed it.
83.3   The question mark, exclamation point, or the dash are placed outside the quotation marks unless it is part of the quotation:
            Did he say, "I will see you home"?
            He asked, "May I see you home?"

NOW WORK THE EXERCISE ON PAGE 107

Exercise 45

		Right answers for page 105	Your answers for page 107

Trial I   Place R if right; W, if wrong:

1. He told me "that he would not do it." — W–78 ( )
2. Did you ask, "What shall I do?" — R–77.2 ( )
3. "This," he said, "is more than enough!" — W–78 ( )
4. He called me a "tight-wad." — R–80 ( )
5. Longfellow wrote "The Village Blacksmith." — W–79 & 43 ( )
6. He said you should not act so." — R–77.3 ( )
7. He answered, "yes," I intend to go. — W–78 ( )
8. He asked, "Have you read Poe's 'The Bells',?" — W–80.1 ( )
9. The crowd arose and sang "The Star Spangled Banner." — W–78 ( )
10. He answered, "I heard him say, 'I did it!'" — W–77.4 ( )
11. She replied "that she would be happy to accept." — W–77.6 ( )
12. He told her, "I shall always remember this hour!" — R–79 ( )
13. He said, "Don't run away"; I agreed with him. — R–73.14 ( )
14. "This," he said, "is what I told him: 'Go directly to the general and tell him, "I will volunteer!"'" — R–74 / W–60.11 ( )
15. "James!" a voice called from the hall. — R–69 ( )

CHECK your answers with the right ones on page 109. If you miss none, go ahead. If you miss one or more, try

W–71
W–60.15   _____
R–75.4   Number
W–62   wrong
R–70.2

Trial II   Place R if right; W, if wrong:

1. "I hope," he said that you will go. — R–72 ( )
2. He played the banjo and sang "Home on the Range." — R–70.1 ( )
3. "Hurricane" Thompson sternly looked at him. — R–71 ( )
4. He asked meekly, "May I come in"? — R–75.2 ( )
5. "I will go," he replied; "but John must stay." — W–69 ( )
6. He said, "I heard him cry, 'Get out of here! — R–74 ( )
7. He called her "cute," and she really was. — R–73.13 ( )
8. Have you read Poe's "The Raven?" — R–75.1 ( )
9. "Now," said he, "did he say, 'I promise to help you!'"? — R–75.3 ( )
10. "I may go," replied Jane, but don't count on me. ( )
11. This is the chapter he wrote: "Early American Policy." ( )
12. The group sang "Home, Sweet Home." ( )
13. He said "that he hoped we would succeed." ( )
14. The girls said he was a "square." ( )
15. He declared that you were dead wrong. ( )

AFTER MASTERY, TURN TO PAGE 108

_____
Number
wrong

Hints: Italics — Punctuation

84.0 Italic type slants. If the writer wishes to direct the printer to set a word in italic type, he underscores the word once. The difference in appearance makes italics a mark of emphasis. When in doubt whether to use quotation marks or italics, use quotation marks in informal writing and italics in formal.

Hint 84. Use italics to identify complete or separate publications.
As stated in 81.5, quotation marks are used for the *parts* of these publications. Thus we speak of "Rip Van Winkle" in *The Sketch Book*.

- 84.1 Books: *The Scarlet Letter*.
- 84.2 Magazines and newspapers: *The Columbus Dispatch*.
- 84.3 Musical productions: *My Fair Lady*.
- 84.4 Plays: *King Lear*.
- 84.5 Long poems: *Evangeline*.
- 84.6 Works of Art: *The Sistine Madonna*.
- 84.7 Names of ships, trains, aircraft: *The Serapis*.

Hint 85. Use italics for foreign words and phrases.
Examples: He tried to work out the *modus operandi*.
His philosophy neglects the *Weltanschauung*.
The act, as you know, was a *fait accompli*.

Hint 86. Use italics for words, letters, and figures when they are referred to as such.
Examples: Distinguish between *its* and *it's*. Mind your *p's* and *q's*.
Which is right—*your* or *you're*? My *l's* look like *7's*.

Hint 87. Use italics to emphasize a word or phrase.
Formerly writers used capitals and italics to make thoughts emphatic. Modern usage saves both of these for real needs. Thus it is good to avoid an overuse of italics for emphasis. The following examples show proper usage:
I said he *was* a good singer.
Never, *under any conditions*, should you drive after drinking.
I shall love you *always*.

NOW WORK THE EXERCISE ON PAGE 109

Exercise 46

Trial I   Place R if right; W, if wrong:

		Right answers for page 107	Your answers for page 109

1. Many critics consider "David Copperfield" his greatest novel.   W   ( )
2. I read Chapter v, *Home Influences*, in the book, "How to Succeed."   R   ( )
3. He said in irony, "Ohio is a good state to come *from.*"   R   ( )
4. Which word do you mean—*to, too,* or *two?*   R   ( )
5. *Always* dot your *i*'s and cross your *t*'s.   R   ( )
6. He ends too many sentences with *et cetera*.   W   ( )
7. She had a reservation on the "Zephyr," a very fast train.   W   ( )
8. The article, "Our Next President," appeared in *Harper's Magazine*.   W   ( )
9. As a boy I read Stevenson's novel, *Treasure Island*.   R   ( )
10. We ate steak and potatoes "au grautin."   R   ( )
11. I subscribe to *The New York Times*.   W   ( )
12. In New York harbor I saw the liner, "Queen Elizabeth."   R   ( )
13. I paused to await her sad *auf Wiedersehen*.   R   ( )
14. The plural of *woman* is *not* "wimmen."   R   ( )
15. He has read the novel, "Grapes of Wrath."   R   ( )

CHECK your answers with the right ones on page 110. If you miss none, go ahead. If you miss one or more, try

Number wrong

Trial II

1. Have you read the novel, *Vanity Fair?*   ( )
2. "Hiawatha" is a long and great American epic.   W   ( )
3. He had worked out a queer *modus vivendi*.   R   ( )
4. Have you seen Lindbergh's *The Spirit of St. Louis*.   R   ( )
5. *Thoughts* end up in *deeds*.   W   ( )
6. And now we must say, "au revoir."   R   ( )
7. *Always* fasten your seat belt.   W   ( )
8. Chapter 4, "How to Make Friends," is the best chapter in the book.   R   ( )
9. Have you seen the movie, "The Disorderly Orderly"?   W   ( )
10. Do not use *etc.* too frequently.   R   ( )
11. You have missed a pleasant experience if you have not read the book, *Lorna Doone*.   W R   ( )
12. Once is "once" too often.   R   ( )
13. One of our great battleships was the "Constitution."   W   ( )
14. He was lost on the "Lusitania."   R   ( )
15. Our class play will be "The Merchant of Venice."   R   ( )

AFTER MASTERY, TURN TO PAGE 110

Number wrong

Hints: Capitalization   Punctuation

89.0   The modern tendency is to reduce the amount of capitalization. It is a fad with some advertisers and journalists to omit all capitals. Do not adopt this fad. However, it is good advice not to over-capitalize, and when in doubt, don't.

Hint 88. Capitalize the first word of every sentence.
Do the same with every direct quotation, every line of poetry, every line of an outline, the salutation and the complimentary close of a letter.
>   Sentence: He is my hero.
>   Direct quotation: He said, "Give me liberty ...."
>   Poetry: The curfew tolls the knell of parting day.
>   Salutation of a letter: My dear Sir:
>   Complimentary close: Yours truly,

Hint 89. Capitalize proper nouns and words derived from them.
89.1   Thus you would capitalize the following:
  89.11   Persons and places: Mary; George Washington; Newark; Ohio.
  89.12   Political and geographical divisions: The United States; the New England States; Alaska; the Bahama Islands.
  89.13   Historical events, periods, documents: The Civil War; the Middle Ages; the Declaration of Independence.
  89.14   Names of races and languages: English; Caucasian; Jewish.
  89.15   Names of organizations: Red Cross; Republican Party.
  89.16   Days of the week and months: Tuesday; July.
  89.17   Religious terms: God; Bible; Apostles' Creed; Protestant; Christ (Personal pronouns referring to the Deity—He; Thee; Him).
  89.18   Derivatives of proper names: Miltonic; British; Biblical.
  89.19   Abbreviations: B.C.; USNR; Ph.D.; Jr.
    89.191   Personifications: Old Man Winter; Nature; Fate.
    89.192   Names of educational institutions, departments, courses, classes, and degrees: Capital University; the English Department; the Senior Class; French (but not *chemistry*), Bachelor of Science.
    89.193   Trade names: Jello; Wheaties; Chevrolet; Kodak.

Hint 90. Capitalize important words.
Capitalize the titles of themes, articles, pamphlets, books, plays, motion pictures, poems, magazines, newspapers, musical compositions, songs, works of art, etc.
>   Right: *The Tale of Two Cities;* My Fishing Trip; *Hiawatha; Life; The Music Man; The Horse Market.*

90.1   Do not capitalize the names of the seasons, points of the compass unless you use them as special names of a region, names of relatives unless used as a substitute for their proper names, names of general college courses unless they are proper names, names of professions and vocations. Thus these are correct: Next *winter* I am going *south*. Please, *Mother*, let me go. My *mother* is at home. In college I take *history* and *German*. I am studying *chemistry* as I hope to become a *doctor*. I reported to *Doctor* Skelton.

NOW WORK EXERCISE 47

Exercise 47

	Right answers for page 109	Your answers for page 111

Trial I   Place R if right; W, if wrong:

1. I made a donation to the Red Cross.   W   ( )
2. He was born in 90 b.c.   W   ( )
3. In the Fall he went East.   R   ( )
4. He signed his letter, "Yours Truly,"   R   ( )
5. He said, "I shall return."   R   ( )
6. He wrote a letter to my Mother.   R   ( )
7. We salute thee, Spring, in all thy beauty.   W   ( )
8. Tell me not in mournful numbers ....   R   ( )
9. He accepted Christ as Lord and Savior.   R   ( )
10. He belongs to the catholic church.   W   ( )
11. He wishes to earn his a.b. and m.d. at the university.   W   ( )
12. Then Nature smiled her sweetest smile.   W   ( )
13. The Senior Class expects each senior to attend.   R   ( )
14. He is Peter's Uncle.   W   ( )
15. I have tickets for *Hamlet*.   W   ( )

Number wrong ____

CHECK your answers with the right ones on page 113. If you miss none, go ahead. If you miss one or more, try

Trial II   Place R if right; W, if wrong:

1. I live in Columbus, Ohio.   R   ( )
2. Old man winter blew a freezing breath.   W   ( )
3. All are needed by each one.   R   ( )
4. He always signs his letters, "Yours Sincerely,"   R   ( )
5. She received a new bible for Christmas.   R   ( )
6. His father had fought in the Civil War.   W   ( )
7. Please, mother, send me some flowers.   R   ( )
8. He told his Father all about it.   R   ( )
9. Next Summer I am going North to fish.   W   ( )
10. I like to study history and French.   R   ( )
11. He told Doctor Haines, "I want to be a doctor."   R   ( )
12. He died in 55 b.c.   W   ( )
13. She said, "Never speak to me again!"   W   ( )
14. The British can't speak the english language.   W   ( )
15. I don't believe that Bacon wrote Shakespeare's plays.   W   ( )

Number wrong ____

AFTER MASTERY, TURN TO PAGE 112

Hints: Abbreviations / Numbers   Punctuation

91.0   Abbreviations, in general, should be avoided in formal writing. When in doubt, don't abbreviate.

Hint 91. Use only acceptable abbreviations.

91.1   Titles before and after proper names: Mr. Leonard; Dr. J. Brown; Rev. R.E. Black; Jim Jackson, Jr.; Thomas Carson, Ph.D.; Ralph Dawson, Sr.

91.2   The abbreviations *Hon.* for Honorable and *Rev.* for Reverend may be abbreviated only when the first names or initials are used:

    Wrong: Hon. Jones spoke. Rev. Young replied.
    Right: Hon. Richard Jones spoke. Rev. E.A. Young replied.
    Right (formal): The Honorable Richard Jones. The Reverend Edwin A. Young.

91.3   Dates and figures: No. 65; 80 B.C.; A.D. 14; 81,896.

91.4   Latin derivatives: i.e.; etc.; cf.; viz.; vs.

91.5   Agencies and organizations: CBS; TVA; UNESCO; NATO; WRFD.

91.6   Footnotes: Thomas Carlyle, *Reminiscences*, p. 476; Ibid., p. 940;

91.7   The word *and* should not be abbreviated except in the name of firms:

    Wrong: He gave gifts to Mike & me.
    Right: He gave gifts to Mike and me.
    Right: The book is published by Brown & Black, publishers.

Hint 92. Write numbers out when they can be expressed in one or two words.

This is particularly true if these numbers appear only occasionally: fifty acres; seven days; ten dollars.

92.1   Do not begin a sentence with a numeral:

    Wrong: 30 freshmen appeared.
    Right: Thirty freshmen appeared.

92.2   Use numerals for the following:

    Dates: July 4, 1776.
    House and room numbers: 758 Francis Avenue, Columbus, Ohio.
    Highway routes: U.S. Highway 71.
    Measurements: 8½ x 11; 32' x 40'.
    Time: 3:30 p.m.
    Money: 75 cents.
    Telephone numbers; Be 1-7809.
    Footnotes: Chapter xii, p. 46.

NOW WORK EXERCISE ON PAGE 113.

Exercise 48

		Right answers for page 111	Your answers for page 113

Trial I   Place R if right; W, if wrong:

1. 6 of us went to town. — R ( )
2. I talked about bees, birds, and etc. — W ( )
3. Our professor is Mr. James Carson, Ph.D. — W ( )
4. Rev. Wright had the invocation. — W ( )
5. I bought 50 acres of meadowland. — R ( )
6. I live at 640 Euclaire St., Newark, Ohio. — W ( )
7. He bought the hat at Jones & White's haberdashery. — R ( )
8. I earned $50, saved $30, and spent $12.25. — R ( )
9. My telephone number is Bel 1-7809. — R ( )
10. Please give me 3 apples. — W ( )
11. We invited Hon. Adams for dinner. — W ( )
12. The picture will be shown at 10 a.m. and four o'clock. — R ( )
13. His flight was on TWA. — R ( )
14. My FICA tax is not very high. — W ( )
15. 2 men and 3 women attended the convention. — R ( )

CHECK your answers with the right ones on page 115. If you miss none, go ahead. If you miss one or more, try

_____ Number wrong

Trial II   Place R if right; W, if wrong:

1. He gave gifts to Jane & Mary. — R ( )
2. 3 men joined our expedition. — W ( )
3. Hon. Morris addressed us. — R ( )
4. I bought 12 head of oxen. — W ( )
5. Our prof is Dr. Paul Keller, Ph.D. — W ( )
6. He came at 7:00 a.m., and returned at two o'clock. — R ( )
7. The right date is June 11, 1965. — W ( )
8. Mr. and Mrs. Robert Whiley visited us. — W ( )
9. I sometimes fly on TWA. — W ( )
10. He gave 75 cents; John gave 30 cents; and I gave 10 cents. — R ( )
11. My address is 161 Short St., Columbus 15, Ohio. — R ( )
12. I needed help, money, friends, and etc. — W ( )
13. This event occurred 55 B.C.; the other, A.D. 30. — R ( )
14. 3 boys and 5 ladies responded. — W ( )
15. I think $52,461,758 is a large amount. — R ( )

AFTER MASTERY, TURN TO PAGE 114

_____ Number wrong

[113]

Review   Punctuation

Let's check our study!

Review all errors and difficulties since the last test.

Grade yourself on your first attempt, using our scale. You will recall it looks like this:

ERRORS	GRADE
0 - 2	A
3 - 4	B
5 - 6	C
7 - 8	D
More than 8	F, or failed

If you make an A or even a B, you are making good progress. If your grade is C or lower, you need to review and re-study to the point of mastery.

Note the right answers in the Key on page 117 and references to the Hints for each error.

NOW TAKE THE TEST ON PAGE 115.
(We are on your side!)

Review Test VIII

		Right answers for page 113	Your answers for page 115

Review Test VIII   Place R if right; W, if wrong:

		Right	Your
1.	Ralph replied, I shall do as you say."	W	( )
2.	Mary said "that her teacher gave her an A."	W	( )
3.	The professor said I should quit "pussy-footing."	R	( )
4.	He answered, "I know he said, Go to work."	W	( )
5.	He asked, "When shall I call"?	W	( )
6.	John Steinbeck wrote the novel, *The Grapes of Wrath*.	R	( )
7.	I will never give it back—*never!*	R	( )
8.	Do these three words trouble you—*to, too, two?*	R	( )
9.	My telephone number is 231-7809.	R	( )
10.	11 men on a team is not enough.	W	( )
11.	She sent a cake to Fred & me.	W	( )
12.	Rev. Tower preached a beautiful sermon.	W	( )
13.	He wrote a note to my Father.	R	( )
14.	The page was 8½ by 11.	R	( )
15.	The french did not like the english.	W	( )
16.	He was a solicitor for the Red Cross.		( )
17.	Old Man Winter puffed and puffed.		( )
18.	Our class play was "Hamlet."		( )
19.	Then he said, "I know you asked, 'When do we eat?'"		( )
20.	He sold me 5 books.		( )
21.	This was *too* much!		( )
22.	He said, "Get out of here"!	W	( )
23.	It happened Sept. 20, 1964.	W	( )
24.	He said "that he would never speak to me again."	W	( )
25.	Read "Rip Van Winkle" in Irving's *Sketch Book*.	W	( )
26.	In college I took chemistry, Greek, and history.	W	( )
27.	Its a shame that somebody broke it's cover.	W	( )
28.	Hon. Scott is a Democrat.	R	( )
29.	This battle happened 15 B.C.	R	( )
30.	I refer you to the Reverend John Brown, D.D.	R	( )

AFTER MASTERY, TURN TO PAGE 116

R
R
W
R
W
R

Number wrong

Grade ___

Hints: Spelling

Spelling

93.0 Spelling in English is difficult because English has adopted words with their peculiar spellings and pronunciations from other languages. For this reason we do not pronounce certain words as they are spelled. Rules often are not a safe guide because of the many exceptions.
We have simplified our treatment to a few Hints.

Hint 93. Build your own personal list of spelling demons.
Add to this list as your vocabulary grows. Work for mastery with this list.

Hint 94. Write correctly seven times each word you have misspelled.
This practice is not a penalty. Writing is really automatic, unconscious muscular reaction to ideas that must be expressed. Substitute a right habit for a wrong one.

Hint 95. Use memory devices to help you remember the correct spelling.
These memory devices are called *mnemonic devices*. Here are some: l-i-c-e for be*lie*ve and rec*ei*ve; a princi*pal* (main teacher) is a *pal;* a princi*ple* is a ru*le;* se*par*ate from the Latin word, *pars,* a part.

Hint 96. Get the dictionary habit.
Whenever you have the least doubt about the spelling of a word, check it in your dictionary.

FIFTY WORDS DIFFICULT TO SPELL

1. absence
2. academic
3. accommodate
4. aggressive
5. argument
6. athlete
7. believe
8. benefit
9. business
10. conscientious
11. disappear
12. ecstasy
13. embarrass
14. familiar
15. fulfill
16. government
17. grammar
18. height
19. indispensable
20. insistence
21. irresistible
22. knowledge
23. laboratory
24. necessary
25. niece
26. occasion
27. occurred
28. paralyze
29. permissible
30. perseverance
31. preceding
32. proceed
33. professor
34. psychology
35. receive
36. restaurant
37. rhythm
38. sacrilegious
39. seize
40. separate
41. sergeant
42. subtle
43. superintendent
44. sophomore
45. supersede
46. synonym
47. truly
48. tragedy
49. villain
50. weird

NOW WORK EXERCISE 49

Exercise 49

		Right answers for page 115	Your answers for page 117
Trial I	Place R if right; W, if wrong:		
1.	I believe in the justice of her cause.	W–81	( )
2.	The principle called his teachers together.	W–81	( )
3.	My niece is very attractive.	R–81.6	( )
4.	There were thirty sophmores in the group.	W–82	( )
5.	Is all this noise neccesary?	W–83	( )
6.	Grammer ain't done me no good!	R–84.1	( )
7.	I have faith in our goverment.	R–87	( )
8.	When has this occurred?	R–86	( )
9.	Please seize it and separate it from the others.	R–92.2	( )
10.	Are such actions permissable?	W–92.1	( )
11.	The villain told a weird story.	W–91.7	( )
12.	He is a very suttle superintendant.	W–91.2	( )
13.	Your actions embarrass me.	W–90.1	( )
14.	I acquired this knowledge in the laboratory.	R–92.2	( )
15.	That motel can't acommodate them.	W–89.14	( )

CHECK your answers with the right ones on page 119. If you missed none, go ahead. If you missed one or more try

		R–89.15	
		R–89.191	Number wrong
		W–84.4	
		R–82	
Trial II	Place R if right; W, if wrong:	W–92	
		R–87	
1.	My proffessor thinks I'm a poor speller.	W–83	( )
2.	His basic principal is never to agree.	R–92.2	( )
3.	I like rhyme and I like rhythm.	W–81	( )
4.	My grammer is better than my arithmetic.	R–84.1	( )
5.	Absence makes the hart grow fonder.	R–89.192	( )
6.	He was preceeding the band.	W–78	( )
7.	This act was really sacrilegious.	W–91.2	( )
8.	I ordered a turkey dinner at the restrunt.	R–89.19	( )
9.	This was unnecessary on this happy occasion.	R–91.2	( )
10.	I believe he will receive the nomination.		( )
11.	That was a weird way to seize it.		( )
12.	He won the arguement.		( )
13.	Let us procede as we planned.		( )
14.	Separate the sheep from the goats.		( )
15.	His insistence was irresistible.		( )

AFTER MASTERY, TURN TO PAGE 118.

Number wrong

Hints: Word Usage

Hint 98. Read widely.
As you read, note new and precise words and add them to your own vocabulary. Use a good, new word three times and it is yours.

Hint 99. Use the right word.
In speaking or writing, don't be sloppy. Don't use just any word. Use the precise word. Use the exact word. A thesaurus (a book of synonyms and antonyms) could help.

Hint 100. Use your dictionary.
By this time you should realize how precious a book your dictionary is. It is a treasure house of valuable information about words. In addition to spelling, syllabication, meaning, and pronunciation, it tells you of the origin and development of words (etymology), the level of language to which these words belong, and may indicate their synonyms (same meanings) and antonyms (opposite meanings). Wide reading will give you the connotation (coloring) of words, but only your dictionary can provide you with their proper denotation.
Here is

A SHORT LIST OF TROUBLESOME WORDS

accept, except	lose, loose
affect, effect	off of
already, all ready	ought to of
among, between	practical, practicable
can, may	principal, principle
continual, continuous	raise, rise
each other, one another	sit, set
enthuse	so
farther, further	sure, surely
fine, nice, cute	teach (transitive)
fix	than, then
hanged, hung	their, there, they're
have got	this here, that here
healthy, healthful	those kind
in, into	to, too, two
is when, is where, is because	try and
its, it's	used to could
later, latter	way, ways
learn (intransitive)	where at
lie, lay	would of
leave, let	you all
less, fewer	

NOW WORK THE EXERCISE ON PAGE 119

Exercise 50

	Right answers for page 117	Your answers for page 119
Trial I Place R if right; W, if wrong:		
1. This here book is good reading.	R	( )
2. His contribution is smaller then mine.	W	( )
3. She will not except him as her suitor.	R	( )
4. They hanged the thief on an apple tree.	W	( )
5. If I had known, I would of gone.	W	( )
6. He fell off of the roof.	W	( )
7. I don't do as well as I used to could.	W	( )
8. He hates those kind of concerts.	R	( )
9. They're going, but there wasn't enough room in their car.	R	( )
10. She was all ready there.	W	( )
11. These two men were too kind to me.	R	( )
12. Between the three of us, what do you think?	W	( )
13. I fear he will loose that wallet.	R	( )
14. Coaching is when you give advice to the team.	R	( )
15. He learned me all I know.	W	( )
		Number wrong

CHECK your answers with the right ones on Page 121. If you missed none, go ahead. If you missed one or more, try

Trial II Place R if right; W, if wrong:		
1. The shed was between the two barns.	W	( )
2. The farther he went, the easier it was.	W	( )
3. That there hat costs ten dollars.	R	( )
4. His yard is larger then ours.	W	( )
5. All went except him.	W	( )
6. He hung his clothes on a hickory limb.	W	( )
7. If I'd a-knowed, I would of went.	R	( )
8. She likes those kind of colors.	W	( )
9. Their they were without there car.	R	( )
10. Now we are all ready.	R	( )
11. The cost was two dollars too much.	R	( )
12. His failure is because he wasted too much money.	W	( )
13. He jumped down off the roof.	W	( )
14. What would you lose by this transaction?	R	( )
15. He never learned me to do anything at all.	R	( )
		Number wrong

AFTER MASTERY, TURN TO PAGE 120

The Home Stretch

We have almost finished our workbook.

We hope it has given you help and insight in your English.

Of course you will want to take a FINAL EXAMINATION and give yourself a grade.

We suggest that you review your errors on all eight of the preceding tests. Be sure you understand the right answers.

The Final Examination consists of two parts:

The first (and here you may be surprised!) consists of the TRIAL TEST, page 3. Cover your previous answers with a slip of paper and take this test again, writing your answers on this slip. Check your answers with the Key on page 123 and designate the number wrong in the blank below.

The second is the Final Examination, Part II, page 121. Take it and then check your answers with the right ones on page 123. Then designate the number wrong in the blank below. Add the number wrong for each test and grade yourself according to this scale:

ERRORS	GRADE	NUMBER WRONG
0 - 4	A	TEST I _____
5 - 8	B	TEST II _____
9 - 12	C	TOTAL _____ GRADE _____
13 - 16	D	
More than 16	F, or failed (Ouch! I shudder at the thought!)	

Final Examination, Part II

		Right answers for page 119	Your answers for page 121
Final Examination, Part II Place R if right; W, if wrong:			
1.	After this great task had been accomplished.	W	( )
2.	She answered sourly, "It tastes sour."	W	( )
3.	He sure swam good.	W	( )
4.	Brutus is an honorable man.	R	( )
5.	He ate bread, milk and honey (three items).	W	( )
6.	He called for my parents were expecting him.	W	( )
7.	Its on it's way to it's destination.	W	( )
8.	The boys' chorus outnumbered the girls'.	W	( )
9.	Who's hat are you wearing?	R	( )
10.	She is, well, rather fond of me.	W	( )
11.	At this station there were 7,546 soldiers.	R	( )
12.	The house which he built for his bride is modern.	W	( )
13.	After I had hesitated a long time, I replied to him.	W	( )
14.	My 3's look like my 8's.	W	( )
15.	I have a well-worn volume of Keats' poems.	W	( )
16.	Inside the bear was clawing at the door.		( )
17.	He landed safe because he landed safely.		( )
18.	If you had asked, I would of gone.		( )
19.	I have went home.		( )
20.	That he played beautifully is evident.		( )
21.	Stop and then you should look and listen.		( )
22.	Have you read any of Demosthenes's orations?	R	( )
23.	The height of the mountains astonish the beholder.	R	( )
24.	He buys at the co-op.	W	( )
25.	I read "Rip Van Winkle" in Irving's *Sketch Book*.	W	( )
26.	He replied, "I know he asked, 'What shall I do?' "	R	( )
27.	He struck, but misses the ball.	R	( )
28.	Math, English, Latin; these give me the most trouble.	W	( )
29.	The man, who hesitates, is lost.	W	( )
30.	I lay on the couch yesterday.	W	( )
31.	His entering the room caused the confusion.	R	( )
32.	If I were chairman, I would report.	R	( )
		W	
CHECK your answers with the right ones on Page 123.		R	
		R	Number wrong
		W	

Index

All numbers refer to pages

Abbreviations, *112*
Absolute phrase, *58*
Abstract noun, *18*
Active Voice, *44*
Adjective, *4, 58*
Adjective clauses, *60*
Adverbs, *4, 60*
Adverbial clauses, *60*
Adverbial phrases, *58*
Agreement of pronoun with antecedent, *22*
Agreement of subject and predicate, *40*
Antecedent, *22*
Antonyms, *118*
Apostrophe, *102*
Appositive, *22*
Auxiliary verbs, *32*

Balanced sentence, *76*
Be, conjugation, *125*
Brackets, *98*
But as preposition, *26*

Capitalization, *110*
Case, nominative, *26*
    objective, *26*
    possessive, *26*
Choose, conjugation, *126*
Clauses, *60*
Close punctuation, *90*
Coherence, *76*
Collective noun, *18*
Colon, *86*
Concrete noun, *18*
Condition contrary to fact, *42*
Comma, enclosing, *92*
Comma, separating, *90*
Comma splice, *10*
Common noun, *18*
Comparative degree, *66*
Comparison, *66*
Comparisons, illogical, *68*
Conjugation, *36, 125–127*
Conjunctions, *70*
    coordinating, *70*
    subordinating, *70*
Conjunctive adverbs, *70*
Coordinate conjunctions, *70*
Complements, *14*
Complex sentence, *6*
Complimentary close, letter, *92*

Compound sentence, *6*
Compound-complex sentence, *6*
Compound word, *100*
Correlatives, *70*

Dangling modifiers, *56*
Dash, *88*
Declension, *20*
Degree, *66*
Demonstrative pronouns, *20*
Dependent clauses, *60*
Dictionary, *116, 118*
Direct object, *14*
Division of words, *100*
Double comparative, *66*
Double negative, *68*

Elliptical clauses, *60*
Elliptical periods, *82*
Emphasis, *108*
Exclamation point, *84*

Figures of speech, *76*
For, punctuation, *90*
Foreign words and phrases, *108*
Fragments, *8*
Fused sentence, *12*

Gender, *18*
Genitive, *28*
Gerund, *48 50*
Gerund phrase, *58*
Gerund, with possessive, *50*

Hyphen, *100*

I, overworked, *24*
Idioms, *74*
Illiterate pronouns, *24*
Illogical comparisons, *68*
Imperative mood, *42*
Indefinite pronoun, *20*
Indicative mood, *42*
Indirect object, *14*
Infinitive, *48*
    dangling, *54*
    split, *52*
Inflection, *26*
Interjection, *4, 74*
Interrogation point, *84*

Index

All numbers refer to pages

Interrogative pronoun, *20*
Intransitive verb, *14*
Italics, *108*
It's me, 26
Its, It's, 102

Lay, lie, 38
Lie, lay, 38
Linking verbs, *32*
Like, as, as if, 72
Loose sentence, *76*

Metaphor, *76*
Modifiers, misplaced, *56*
Modifiers, restrictive and nonrestrictive, *62*
Mnemonic devices, *116*
Mood, mode, *42*

Names, capitalization, *110*
Neither, nor, 70
Nominative case, *26*
    subject, subjective complement, *26*
Nonrestrictive clauses, *62*
Nonrestrictive phrases, *62*
Nouns, *18*
Noun clause, *60*
Number, *18*
Numbers, *112*

Objective complement, *14*
Object of preposition, *14*
Of for *have,* 32
Only, its position, *56*
Open punctuation, *90*

Parallelism, *76*
Parallel structure, *76*
Parentheses, *98*
Participle, *34, 48, 50*
Participial phrase, *58*
Parts of speech, *4*
Passive voice, *44*
Period, *80*
Periodic sentence, *76*
Person, *20*
Personal pronoun, *20*
Phrases, *58*
Plurals, *18*
Positive degree, *66*
Possessive case, *28*
Predicate, *6*
Prepositional phrase, *58*

Right answers Trial Test page 3	Right answers Part II page 121
R–26.1	W–3.1
R–27.9	R–6.32
W–93	W–1.5
R–68.13	R–6.31
W–23.4	W–66
	W–65
W–6.12	W–78
R–26.5	R–77.2
W–40	W–78
R–19.5	R–68.11
R–26.3	R–68.23
	R–37.1
R–83.3	R–63
W–50.4	R–80
W–46	R–77.3
R–93	W–65
W–3.2	R–21
	W–22
W–19.1	W–23.4
R–7.9	R–36.6
R–26.1	W–28
W–19.2	W–77.3
W–10.6	W–27.1
	R–75.3
R–10.4	R–84
W–33.3	R–82 & 83
W–32	W–25
W–93	W–62
W–60 & 66	W–37.1
	R–26.1
W–11	R–31.3
W–27.5	R–28.3
R–19.1	
W–34.4	
W–65	
R–32	
R–19.2	

Index

All numbers refer to pages

Preposition, *74*
Principal parts of verbs, *34*
Progressive form of verb, *36*
Pronoun, *20*
Proper noun, *18*
Punctuation, *80*

Question, indirect, *84*
Question mark, *84*
Quotation marks, *106*
    double, *106*
    single, *106*

Reciprocal pronoun, *20*
Reflexive pronoun, *20*
Restrictive clause, *62*
Retained object, *44*
Rhetorical punctuation, *80*
Run-on sentence, *12*

Salutation, letter, *86*
Semicolon, *96*
Sentence fragment, *8*
Sentence, fused, *12*
Sentence, meaning, *6*
Sentence, structure, *6*
Sentence, style, *76*
Shall and *will*, *38*
Shifts, *36, 42*
Simple sentence, *6*
Sit, set, *38*
So, misuse, *72*
Spelling, *116*
Split infinitive, *52*
Squinting modifiers, *56*
Strong verbs, *34*
Subject of sentence, *6*
Subjective complement, *14*

Subjunctive mood, *42*
Subordinate clause, *60*
Subordinating conjunctions, *72*
Superlative degree, *66*
Syllabication, *100*
Synonyms, *118*

Tense, *36*
There, expletive, *40*
Those kind, *22*
To, too, two, *118*
Transitive verb, *14*
Triple construction, *76*

Unity, *76*

Variety, *76*
Verbals, *48*
    gerunds, *48*
    infinitives, *48*
    participles, *48*
Verbals, dangling, *54*
Verb, intransitive, *14*
Verbs, *14*
Verbs, auxiliary, *32*
Verbs, linking, *32*
Verbs, principal parts, *34*
Verbs, regular, *34*
Verbs, strong, *34*
Voice, *44*
    active, *44*
    passive, *44*

Weak verbs, *34*
Well, *4*
Wish, request, subjunctive mood, *42*
Word usage, *118*

Conjugation of **to be** — Appendix

Table I: Conjugation of to be
Principal Parts: be, was, been

ACTIVE VOICE

INDICATIVE MOOD

	Singular	Plural

PRESENT TENSE

	Singular	Plural
1st person	I am	we are
2nd person	you are	you are
3rd person	he is	they are

PAST TENSE

	Singular	Plural
1st person	I was	we were
2nd person	you were	you were
3rd person	he was	they were

FUTURE TENSE

	Singular	Plural
1st person	I shall be	we shall be
2nd person	you will be	you will be
3rd person	he will be	they will be

PRESENT PERFECT TENSE

	Singular	Plural
1st person	I have been	we have been
2nd person	you have been	you have been
3rd person	he has been	they have been

PAST PERFECT TENSE

	Singular	Plural
1st person	I had been	we had been
2nd person	you had been	you had been
3rd person	he had been	they had been

FUTURE PERFECT TENSE

	Singular	Plural
1st person	I shall have been	we shall have been
2nd person	you will have been	you will have been
3rd person	he will have been	they will have been

SUBJUNCTIVE MOOD (reluctantly disappearing)

PRESENT TENSE

	Singular	Plural
1st person	(if) I be	(if) we be
2nd person	(if) you be	(if) you be
3rd person	(if) he be	(if) they be

PAST TENSE

	Singular	Plural
1st person	(if) I were	(if) we were
2nd person	(if) you were	(if) you were
3rd person	(if) he were	(if) they were

IMPERATIVE MOOD
Present Tense

be (you)   be (you)

VERBALS

Present infinitive: to be   Perfect infinitive: to have been
Present participle: being   Past participle: been
                                   Perfect participle: having been

Present gerund: being   Perfect gerund: having been

Appendix

Conjugation of **choose**

Table II: Conjugation of choose
Principal parts: choose, chose, chosen

<table>
<tr><td colspan="3" align="center">ACTIVE VOICE</td><td colspan="2" align="center">PASSIVE VOICE</td></tr>
<tr><td colspan="5" align="center">INDICATIVE MOOD</td></tr>
<tr><td colspan="5" align="center">PRESENT TENSE</td></tr>
<tr><td></td><td>Singular</td><td>Plural</td><td>Singular</td><td>Plural</td></tr>
<tr><td>1st person</td><td>I choose</td><td>we choose</td><td>I am chosen</td><td>we are chosen</td></tr>
<tr><td>2nd person</td><td>you choose</td><td>you choose</td><td>you are chosen</td><td>you are chosen</td></tr>
<tr><td>3rd person</td><td>he chooses</td><td>they choose</td><td>he is chosen</td><td>they are chosen</td></tr>
<tr><td colspan="5" align="center">PAST TENSE</td></tr>
<tr><td>1st person</td><td>I chose</td><td>we chose</td><td>I was chosen</td><td>we were chosen</td></tr>
<tr><td>2nd person</td><td>you chose</td><td>you chose</td><td>you were chosen</td><td>you were chosen</td></tr>
<tr><td>3rd person</td><td>he chose</td><td>they chose</td><td>he was chosen</td><td>they were chosen</td></tr>
<tr><td colspan="5" align="center">FUTURE TENSE</td></tr>
<tr><td>1st person</td><td>I shall choose</td><td>we shall choose</td><td>I shall be chosen</td><td>we shall be chosen</td></tr>
<tr><td>2nd person</td><td>you will choose</td><td>you will choose</td><td>you will be chosen</td><td>you will be chosen</td></tr>
<tr><td>3rd person</td><td>he will choose</td><td>they will choose</td><td>he will be chosen</td><td>they will be chosen</td></tr>
<tr><td colspan="5" align="center">PRESENT PERFECT TENSE</td></tr>
<tr><td>1st person</td><td>I have chosen</td><td>we have chosen</td><td>I have been chosen</td><td>we have been chosen</td></tr>
<tr><td>2nd person</td><td>you have chosen</td><td>you have chosen</td><td>you have been chosen</td><td>you have been chosen</td></tr>
<tr><td>3rd person</td><td>he has chosen</td><td>they have chosen</td><td>he has been chosen</td><td>they have been chosen</td></tr>
<tr><td colspan="5" align="center">PAST PERFECT TENSE</td></tr>
<tr><td>1st person</td><td>I had chosen</td><td>we had chosen</td><td>I had been chosen</td><td>we had been chosen</td></tr>
<tr><td>2nd person</td><td>you had chosen</td><td>you had chosen</td><td>you had been chosen</td><td>you had been chosen</td></tr>
<tr><td>3rd person</td><td>he had chosen</td><td>they had chosen</td><td>he had been chosen</td><td>they had been chosen</td></tr>
<tr><td colspan="5" align="center">FUTURE PERFECT TENSE</td></tr>
<tr><td>1st person</td><td>I shall have chosen</td><td>we shall have chosen</td><td>I shall have been chosen</td><td>we shall have been chosen</td></tr>
<tr><td>2nd person</td><td>you will have chosen</td><td>you will have chosen</td><td>you will have been chosen</td><td>you will have been chosen</td></tr>
<tr><td>3rd person</td><td>he will have chosen</td><td>they will have chosen</td><td>he will have been chosen</td><td>they will have been chosen</td></tr>
</table>

SUBJUNCTIVE MOOD (reluctantly disappearing)

PRESENT TENSE
Singular: (if) I, you, he choose   (if) I, you, he be chosen
Plural: (if) we, you, they choose   (if) we, you, they be chosen

PAST TENSE
Singular: (if) I, you, he chose   (if) I, you, he were chosen
Plural: (if) we, you, they chose   (if) we, you, they were chosen

IMPERATIVE MOOD

choose (you)   be chosen (you)

[126]

Appendix

(Table II: Conjugation of choose)

VERBALS

ACTIVE		PASSIVE
	INFINITIVES	
Present tense: to choose		to be chosen
Perfect tense: to have chosen		to have been chosen
	PARTICIPLES	
Present tense: choosing		being chosen
Past tense: (none)		chosen
Perfect tense: having chosen		having been chosen
	GERUNDS	
Present tense: choosing		being chosen
Past tense: (none)		(none)
Perfect tense: having chosen		having been chosen